Bannockburn 1314

Robert Bruce's great victory

Campaign • 102

Bannockburn 1314

Robert Bruce's great victory

Pete Armstrong · Illustrated by Graham Turner
Series editor Lee Johnson · *Consultant editor* David G Chandler

First published in Great Britain in 2002 by Osprey Publishing,
Midland House, West Way, Botley, Oxford OX2 0PH, UK
443 Park Avenue South, New York, NY 10016, USA
Email: info@ospreypublishing.com

CIP Data for this publication is available from the British Library

ISBN 978-1-85532-609-5

Editor: Lee Johnson
Design: The Black Spot
Index by Alan Rutter
Maps by The Map Studio
3D bird's eye views by John Plumer
Battlescene artwork by Graham Turner
Originated by PPS Grasmere Ltd., Leeds, UK
Printed in China through World Print Ltd.
Typeset in Helvetica Neue and ITC New Baskerville

08 09 10 11 12 16 15 14 13 12 11 10 9 8 7

FOR A CATALOGUE OF ALL BOOKS PUBLISHED BY
OSPREY PLEASE CONTACT:

NORTH AMERICA
Osprey Direct, C/o Random House Distribution Center,
400 Hahn Road, Westminster, MD 21157, USA
E-mail: info@ospreydirect.com

ALL OTHER REGIONS
Osprey Direct UK, P.O. Box 140, Wellingborough,
Northants, NN8 2FA, UK
E-mail: info@ospreydirect.co.uk

www.ospreypublishing.com

Artist's note

Readers may care to note that the original paintings from
which the colour plates in this book were prepared
are available for private sale. All reproduction copyright
whatsoever is retained by the Publishers. All enquiries
should be addressed to:

Graham Turner
P.O. Box 568,
Aylesbury,
Bucks HP17 8ZX
United Kingdom
www.studio88.co.uk

The Publishers regret that they can enter into no
correspondence upon this matter.

KEY TO MILITARY SYMBOLS

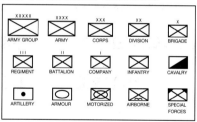

CONTENTS

ORIGINS OF THE CAMPAIGN

On a stormy night in 1286, Alexander III of Scotland set out to ride to his manor of Kinghorn to be with his new wife, the beautiful Yolande de Dreux. In the darkness his horse stumbled on a cliff-top path and at dawn he was found with a broken neck at the foot of the cliffs. Scotland was without a king and the golden age of peace and prosperity that Scotland had enjoyed under Alexander was drawing to a close. Alexander's first wife Margaret, daughter of Henry III of England, died in 1275 having borne three children, two sons and a daughter, who were all dead by 1284, leaving the succession in jeopardy. It had been hoped that Alexander's marriage to the young French woman would produce a male heir to rectify the situation, instead, his sudden death left his sickly three-year-old granddaughter Margaret as heir. The child's mother, the queen of Eric II of Norway, died in 1283 giving birth to Margaret, 'The Maid of Norway', last of the royal house of Canmore. A council of regency consisting of six guardians of the realm was appointed to administer Scotland in the name of little Queen Margaret in far away Norway.

In England, King Edward I, as strong and able a king as ever ruled Scotland's powerful southern neighbour, pondered the implications of the death of his brother-in-law. He realised that the possibility of controlling Scotland, as he did Wales and Ireland, was within his grasp and that would make him ruler of the British Isles. He proposed a marriage between his two-year-old son, Edward of Caernarvon, and the Maid of Norway. The Scots assented warily, but insisted, through the terms of the treaty of Birgham, that though there was to be a union of the two crowns, the realm of Scotland was to continue as an entirely separate and independent kingdom. The Maid of Norway set sail for Scotland but became ill on the voyage and died soon after landing in Orkney, leaving the question of the Scottish succession open again.

There was no shortage of claimants to the Crown of Scotland. Two of them – John Balliol and Robert Bruce, 5th Lord of Annandale, known as the 'Competitor' – were descended from the Scottish King David I's grandson, David, Earl of Huntingdon. The Scots asked Edward I to arbitrate between the 14 'competitors' for the vacant throne. At Berwick in November 1292 he decided in favour of John Balliol, who was connected to the powerful Comyn family, bitter rivals of the Bruces. King John rendered homage to Edward I for his kingdom and was subsequently repeatedly humiliated by him as he sought to underline his dominance over the Scots. By 1295 the exasperated Scots lords had had enough, and they persuaded Balliol to renounce his allegiance to the English King and sign a treaty with the French that initiated the auld alliance. Predictably, Edward invaded Scotland the following year and crushed the ineptly led Scots at the battle of Dunbar. John Balliol surrendered his kingdom and as a final indignity Edward tore the Royal Arms from his surcoat before despatching him to the Tower of London; thus the unfortunate Balliol earned the nickname 'Toom Tabard' (empty coat).

Wallace's Rebellion

At the end of 1296 Edward returned south, taking the Stone of Destiny from Scone with him to Westminster and leaving his well-garrisoned northern conquest in the hands of the Earl of Surrey. Disturbances broke out almost immediately, and in May 1297 William Wallace murdered the English Sheriff of Lanark, an act that propelled Wallace into the spotlight of Scottish history and sparked open rebellion in the land. In September, at Stirling Bridge, Wallace defeated an English force under Surrey and further fanned the flames of revolt in Scotland. His victory resulted in his elevation to the guardianship of the realm and he became effectively, with the support of the people and consent of the church, ruler of Scotland. In 1298 Edward, in vengeful mood, invaded Scotland with a powerful army to hammer the Scots into submission and decisively defeated Wallace at the battle of Falkirk. He resigned the guardianship and disappeared from the pages of history until 1305, when he was betrayed and captured. After a show trial in London he was convicted of treason and dragged to Smithfield, where he was publicly hanged, drawn and quartered.

'King Hobbe'

Robert Bruce could trace his ancestry back beyond Adam Bruce, who came to England with William the Conqueror, to Lodver, the 10th-century Norse Earl of Orkney. Adam's eldest son was the first to be named Robert Bruce and he became one of the great magnates of northern England, with widespread lands in Yorkshire. In 1124 David I, who was his feudal overlord in England, succeeded to the Scottish throne. He wanted to transform Scotland from a backward Celtic society

Statue of William Wallace, made for the Earl of Buchan by John Smith in 1814. It stands in the Scottish Borders not far from the Kirk o' the Forest in Selkirk where Wallace was elected Guardian of Scotland.

An early 14th-century knight armed in his finery for the joust. Such extravagant clothing would have been replaced with more practical garb for a campaign in Scotland. (author's drawing)

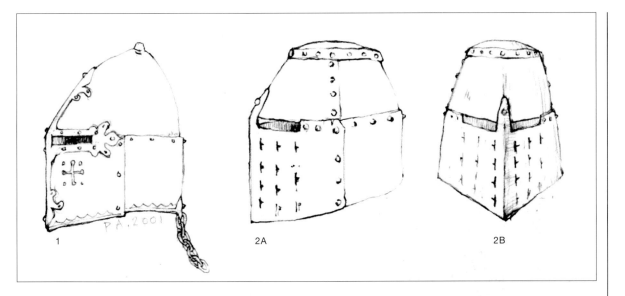

into a modern European state and encouraged Anglo-Norman settlement north of the Border. One of his first acts in pursuance of this policy was to grant his vassal, Robert Bruce, the vast estates of the lordship of Annandale. Thus the Bruces became one of the most powerful families in Scotland.

The loyalties and allegiances of Robert Bruce in the years up to 1306 were shifting and uncertain. In company with many other Scots, he supported Edward I on the outbreak of war in 1296. Bruce's stance was determined partly because the patriotic resistance to Edward was led by the Comyns, bitter rivals of the Bruces for power in Scotland, and because Bruce saw in Edward his best hope of securing the kingship, which he believed to be his by right. Yet in 1298 Bruce, perhaps not

Early 14th-century Helmets.
1. Reconstruction of the helm from the brass of Sir R. de Trumpington c.1289.
2a, 2b. Helm c.1300, probably German, in the Castel San Angelo, Rome. Early 14th-century armour was similar throughout Europe, and Scotland relied heavily on imported arms. (author's drawing)

Memorial erected in 1685 at Burgh-by-Sands to King Edward I, 'The Hammer of the Scots', who died in camp on Burgh Marsh on 7 July 1307. He had been on his way north to once more hammer the intransigent Scots into submission.

entirely for patriotic motives, became joint Guardian of Scotland together with John the 'Red Comyn' when Wallace resigned the guardianship after the disaster of Falkirk. After a violent quarrel with Comyn, Bruce reverted to his English allegiance and was returned to the king's 'peace', or pardoned, by Edward I early in 1302.

On 10 February 1306 Robert Bruce held a meeting with Comyn in the Greyfriars' Church in Dumfries. In the course of the discussion tempers flared into violence and Bruce stabbed his rival, leaving him bleeding beside the altar to be finished off by his henchmen. The sacrilegious murder left Bruce no choice; outlawed by Edward I and excommunicated by the Pope, he claimed the throne of Scotland as the great-great-grandson of David I. With support from a section of the Scottish Church and nobility he was crowned, despite the absence of the Stone of Destiny, at Scone on 25 March. Many Scots lords opposed Bruce. The Comyns and their allies bayed for revenge and many others would have nothing to do with him. Edward I swore that he would bring Scotland to heel. In June 1306 his lieutenant, Aymer de Valence, surprised and dispersed Bruce's army at Methven near Perth. Worse followed. His sisters, his daughter and Elizabeth his queen were captured and delivered into the hands of Edward I. Bruce's brother Neil was captured at the fall of Kildrummy Castle and brutally executed at Berwick. By the end of June Bruce's position had collapsed, his supporters were scattered and 'King Hobbe' as the English mockingly called him was a hunted fugitive. He escaped his pursuers, however, and took a ship to the tiny Isle of Rathlin off the Ulster coast, where he gained a breathing space and set about reorganising his resources.

In early 1307 Bruce and a handful of followers ventured a return to the mainland. They landed near Turnberry Castle in Ayrshire and disappeared into the wild fells and moors of Carrick. Bruce's two younger brothers, Thomas and Alexander, meanwhile sailed for Galloway with an expedition intended to provide support by harrying English communications between Carlisle and Ayr, but things went disastrously wrong. As the Scots landed in Loch Ryan they were ambushed by the MacDowells of Galloway, bitter opponents of the Bruces, and dispersed in bloody confusion. Thomas and Alexander

RIGHT **King Robert's grip on Scotland tightens inexorably as one by one the English strongholds are captured by the Scots and dismantled. By the beginning of the year, outside Lothian, only Bothwell and Stirling castles are still in the invaders' hands.**

The gateway of Carlisle Castle overlooks the walled Border city. In the early 12th century Cumberland was in the hands of the Scot but in 1157 after the death of David I, Henry II reclaimed Cumberland and the castle became once more part of the English Border defences.

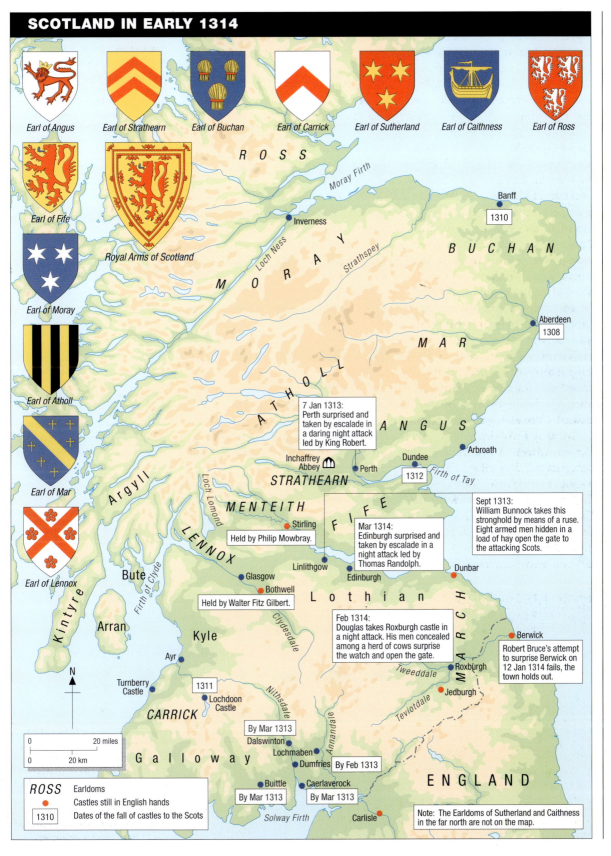

SCOTLAND IN EARLY 1314

Earl of Angus

Earl of Strathearn

Earl of Buchan

Earl of Carrick

Earl of Sutherland

Earl of Caithness

Earl of Ross

Earl of Fife

Royal Arms of Scotland

Earl of Moray

Earl of Atholl

Earl of Mar

Earl of Lennox

R O S S

Moray Firth

Banff
1310

Inverness

B U C H A N

Loch Ness

M O R A Y

Strathspey

Aberdeen
1308

M A R

A T H O L L

7 Jan 1313:
Perth surprised and
taken by escalade in
a daring night attack
led by King Robert.

A N G U S

Arbroath

Inchaffrey
Abbey

Dundee
1312

Perth

Firth of Tay

STRATHEARN

F I F E

Sept 1313:
William Bunnock takes this
stronghold by means of a ruse.
Eight armed men hidden in a
load of hay open the gate to
the attacking Scots.

M E N T E I T H

Mar 1314:
Edinburgh surprised and
taken by escalade in a
night attack led by
Thomas Randolph.

Argyll

Loch Lomond

Stirling

Held by Philip Mowbray.

L E N N O X

Linlithgow

Edinburgh

Dunbar

Bute

Firth of Clyde

Glasgow

Bothwell

L o t h i a n

Held by Walter Fitz Gilbert.

Clydesdale

Feb 1314:
Douglas takes Roxburgh castle in
a night attack. His men concealed
among a herd of cows surprise
the watch and open the gate.

M A R C H

Berwick

Robert Bruce's attempt
to surprise Berwick on
12 Jan 1314 fails, the
town holds out.

Arran

Kintyre

Kyle

Tweeddale

Roxburgh

Ayr

Jedburgh

Teviotdale

N

Turnberry
Castle

1311

Lochdoon
Castle

Nithsdale

Annandale

CARRICK

By Mar 1313

Dalswinton

G a l l o w a y

Lochmaben

Dumfries

By Feb 1313

E N G L A N D

Buittle

By Mar 1313

Caerlaverock

By Mar 1313

Solway Firth

Carlisle

0   20 miles
0   20 km

ROSS Earldoms
● Castles still in English hands
1310 Dates of the fall of castles to the Scots

Note: The Earldoms of Sutherland and Caithness
in the far north are not on the map.

11

Bruce, half dead with wounds, were carted off to Carlisle where Edward I had them hanged and put their heads on display above the town gates. Edward poured troops into southern Scotland, but Bruce's following was growing and in engagements at Glen Trool and Loudon Hill, King Robert had some success against the English. On 7 July 1307 Edward I, the 'Hammer of the Scots', died at Burgh-by-Sands on the Solway and the iron grip in which the Scots had been held in thrall slackened.

ROBERT BRUCE RECOVERS HIS KINGDOM, 1307–1314

Edward I's frivolous son and successor, Edward II, was distracted from the situation in Scotland by his affair with Piers Gaveston and the opposition of his recalcitrant barons (see Opposing Commanders). This allowed Bruce valuable time to deal with his Scottish opponents. He first turned to the south-west and wreaked vengeance on his enemies the MacDowells. Then, leaving James Douglas to complete the subjugation of Galloway, he marched north in September through the Great Glen to confront his arch-rival John Comyn, whose rich earldom of Buchan stretched from Aberdeen to the Moray Firth. Comyn's defeat at Inverurie in May 1308 and his flight south to England, left the earldom at the mercy of King Robert, whose ruthless devastation of the lands of Comyn's supporters became known as the 'herschip of Buchan'. By the summer Bruce had taken Aberdeen and his hold on the north-east was unassailable. By 1309 most of the remaining Scottish opposition to Bruce had been defeated and he turned his attention to driving the English from his kingdom.

Meanwhile, Edward II had patched up a temporary accommodation with his barons and determined to deal with the Scots. He invaded Scotland in 1309 and again in 1310, but the Scots simply melted away

Robert Clifford's mighty stronghold of Brougham Castle stands beside the River Eamont near Penrith. It was built in the early 13th and late 14th centuries and was one of a chain of castles defending the Eden Valley against Scottish incursions.

ABOVE **Sir Robert Clifford's castle at Appleby in the Eden Valley still dominates the old county town of Westmorland.**

LEFT **The fortified church of Newton Arlosh stands close by the medieval fords across the Solway Firth. The tower was built as a defence against Scots raiders in the early 14th century. There are similar fortified church towers at nearby Burgh-by-Sands, Great Salkeld and Penrith.**

before him, avoiding battle and destroying anything of use in their wake, forcing the hungry and dispirited English to withdraw. Edward's costly campaigns achieved little, and inevitably he ran short of cash to pay his troops and had to return south to face the demands of his intransigent barons. At the parliament held in August 1311 Edward was forced to accept all the articles constraining his conduct laid before him by the Lords Ordainers and had to send his favourite into exile in Flanders. But within three months Gaveston returned in secret and fearing the wrath of the barons, hurried north with Edward to take refuge in Scarborough Castle. While the King tried to raise troops elsewhere, Gaveston was besieged by the Earl of Pembroke and in return for a safe conduct he surrendered. As he was being taken south to Pembroke's castle at Wallingford, he was seized by the Earl of Warwick and beheaded on the orders of the Earl of Lancaster.

Robert Bruce took advantage of Edward's distractions and raided the Border counties of England in 1311, leaving a trail of destruction in his

Caerlaverock Castle in Dumfriesshire was besieged and taken by Edward I in 1300; it remained in English hands until it fell to the Scots in 1312. It was 'demolished' by Robert Bruce but soon rebuilt, substantial remains of the original 14th-century masonry can be seen in the present structure. (author's drawing)

wake. During the following summer, with increasing confidence and in greater strength, he struck deep into the Palatinate of Durham. The defenceless northern counties, seeing no hope of succour from Edward II, were forced to purchase a year's truce, giving them immunity from the depredations of the Scots, though they returned to exact further payments of 'blackmail' or protection money the following year and the finances of Bruce's poverty-stricken realm improved accordingly.

In 1309 the English still held a dozen major strongholds in Scotland. These, together with numerous smaller strengths, provided the English with bases from which to dominate the surrounding area. Bruce's strategy was to take and destroy these castles to render them useless to the enemy, as to garrison them himself would have immobilised too much of his limited manpower. Gradually Bruce prised loose the English grasp on Scotland. He had no siege engines so he had to rely on ruses and surprise assaults or, if all else failed, on tedious blockades. At Berwick, Bruce's attempt to take the town by a nocturnal escalade was foiled by a barking dog that alerted the garrison. However, he had more success in January 1313, when the strategically vital town of Perth was surprised and taken in an assault by moonlight.

In south-east Scotland or Lothian, many of the Anglo-Scots of the area held lands on both sides of the Border. Lothian was nominally under English rule, so the inhabitants were obliged to pay 'blackmail' or protection money to Robert Bruce in the same manner as the people of northern England. Many of the smaller castles of Lothian were already in the hands of the Scots when, in February 1314, James Douglas surprised and captured the important castle of Roxburgh. The climax to the campaign against English strongholds in Lothian came the following month when, not to be outdone by Douglas's bold exploit, Thomas Randolph took Edinburgh Castle by escalade in a daring night attack.

CHRONOLOGY

1274

Robert Bruce born at Turnberry Castle, Ayrshire.

1286

Death of King Alexander III of Scotland. His only direct descendant is Margaret the 'Maid of Norway', a three-year-old infant.

1290

The Maid of Norway dies soon after landing in Orkney, triggering a succession crisis. King Edward I of England is invited to arbitrate between the 'Competitors' for the crown of Scotland.

1292

John Balliol is crowned King of Scotland and renders homage to Edward I for his kingdom.

1296

War between England and Scotland begins.
March: Edward I storms and sacks the town of Berwick with much slaughter.
April: Scots routed at the battle of Dunbar. Many Scots lords are sent south to imprisonment in England.
John Balliol submits and resigns his kingdom to Edward I.

1297

11 September: William Wallace and Andrew Moray defeat English at the battle of Stirling Bridge.

1298

Wallace elected Guardian of Scotland.
22 July: Battle of Falkirk. Scots defeated by Edward I. Wallace resigns the Guardianship.

1304

Stirling Castle taken by Edward I.

1305

William Wallace captured.
23 August: Wallace hung, drawn and quartered in London.

1306

10 February: John 'The Red' Comyn murdered by Robert Bruce in the Greyfriars Church, Dumfries.
25 March: Bruce crowned King of Scots at Scone.
19 June: Battle of Methven. Bruce defeated by the Earl of Pembroke.
11 August: Bruce defeated at Dalry by John MacDougal of Argyll.

1307

May: Bruce wins his first significant victory over the Earl of Pembroke at Loudon Hill.
7 July: Edward I dies at Burgh-by-Sands on the Solway coast.

1308

The 'Herschip of Buchan', Bruce devastates the lands of the Earl of Buchan and his supporters following his victory at Inverurie.
August: Bruce defeats John of Lorn at the pass of Brander.

1310

September: Edward II invades Scotland.

1311

Edward II's campaign of 1310–11 proves futile and he withdraws in August.

1312

August: Bruce raids the north of England.

1313

January: Bruce captures Perth.
February: Fall of Dumfries.
May: Bruce takes Isle of Man.

1314

Scots take Roxburgh and Edinburgh. Only Bothwell and Stirling remain in English hands.
17 June: English cross the Tweed at Wark and Coldstream.
22 June: Forward elements of the English army reach Falkirk.
23–24 June: Battle of Bannockburn. Edward II's English army is disastrously defeated by Robert Bruce's Scots.
25 June: Edward II flees to Dunbar and takes ship for Bamburgh in Northumberland.
November: Cambuskenneth Parliament, forfeiture of Bruce's opponents.

1315

Edward Bruce invades Ireland.
July: Siege of Carlisle.

1318

April: Berwick falls to the Scots. Edward Bruce killed at battle of Faughart near Dundalk in Ireland.

1319

Edward II besieges Berwick. Douglas and Moray invade England. 'The Chapter of Myton'.

1320

Declaration of Arbroath.

1322

16 March: Battle of Boroughbridge.
August–September Edward II's last Scottish expedition is a failure.
October 20: Battle of Old Byland.

1327

21 September: Edward II deposed and murdered at Berkeley Castle. His son is crowned as Edward III.

1328

Treaty of Edinburgh ends this phase of the Scottish Wars.

1329

Death of Robert Bruce.

1330

The Good Sir James Douglas killed fighting against the Moors in Spain.

1332

Death of Thomas Randolph, Earl of Moray.

OPPOSING COMMANDERS

THE ENGLISH COMMANDERS

Edward Plantagenet 1284–1327; King Edward II 1307–27

Contemporary chroniclers agree that Edward of Caernarvon was tall, well built, athletic, handsome and brave but also that he was weak-willed, indolent and frivolous, caring neither for politics, war or business but only how to amuse himself. As a youth he cared little for military pursuits and, though he loved horses, field sports and music, his interest in rustic matters such as thatching, hedging and shoeing horses, together with his enthusiasm for rowing and swimming in all weathers, shocked his contemporaries as they were considered improper matters for the attention of a Prince. Edward's constant companion as a youth was Piers Gaveston, the son of a Gascon knight in the service of his father. He was irrepressible, charming and amusing, and it was said that Edward's love for his friend was such that he 'knit an indissoluble bond of affection with him, above all other mortals'. But the bold upstart Gaveston's irreverent insolence towards 'Burst Belly', 'Joseph the Jew' and 'The Black Dog of Arden', as he nicknamed the leading magnates of the realm, earned him their undying hatred. His skill at arms compounded their anger, as he invariably defeated them in encounters in the lists. When Edward of Caernarvon succeeded to the throne in 1307, his first concern was to elevate Piers Gaveston as Earl of Cornwall, a title customarily reserved for royalty. The King's immoderate behaviour and his inability to draw a line between his obsessive involvement with Gaveston and the affairs of state was a folly that drew him increasingly into conflict with his barons and led the country to the brink of civil war. His distraction from events in Scotland allowed Robert Bruce time to establish his position politically and to practically eject the English from his kingdom.

Edward of Caernarvon's first military experience was in 1300

Banner of King Edward II

ABOVE **Banner of King Edward II. (author's drawing)**

ABOVE, RIGHT **King Edward II from his tomb in Gloucester Cathedral. (author's drawing)**

RIGHT **Helm and Crest of King Edward II. (Redrawn by the author from the 14th-century *Armorial de Gelre*)**

17

when, at the age of 16, he and his inseparable companion Gaveston accompanied his father on his campaign in south-west Scotland. Early in 1301 Edward I seemed pleased with his son's conduct and created him Prince of Wales. Later in the same year he entrusted him with an independent command in a two-pronged incursion into Scotland. The experienced Earl of Lincoln guided the Prince's conduct of the expedition but little resulted from it. Edward accompanied his father on his 1303 campaign in Scotland, and he was again in the north in 1306 when he was present at the fall of Kildrummy Castle. Despite Edward's preferences for less military pursuits, his father did not neglect to educate him in military matters nor was he unaware of the realities of campaigning against the Scots. At the beginning of his reign he had experience of Bruce's Fabian strategy in the face of superior forces during his

1310 invasion of Scotland. Edward II may have spent many wearisome days in the saddle pursuing the elusive Scots over moor and bog, but he had no experience of leadership in battle and when the test came he proved quite useless.

Subordinate English Commanders

The Earl of Lancaster and other English magnates of his faction did not answer the King's summons to the muster at Berwick and sent only the very minimum number of men they were obliged to furnish in time of war. Only the Earls of Gloucester, Hereford, Pembroke and Angus answered the summons in person. It is unfair to charge the English leaders with a lack of battlefield experience, as there had not been a major battle in Britain since that of Falkirk in 1298 and the same charge could also be levelled at the Scots leaders. The English, nevertheless, did not want for officers experienced in campaigning against the Scots.

Aymer de Valence, Earl of Pembroke, was tall and pallid of countenance, earning him Gaveston's derisory nickname 'Joseph the Jew'. Though he had opposed Edward's conduct throughout the Gaveston affair, he was essentially a moderate man and a loyal supporter of the King. He was an experienced commander and had campaigned in Scotland in Edward I's time and had defeated Bruce at Methven in 1306. He was Edward II's cousin and, as his lieutenant in Scotland in early 1314, he attended to the organisation of the campaign while awaiting the King's arrival at Berwick. Pembroke's personal retinue included 22 knights and 59 men-at-arms in 1314. The Earl, despite his experience, was not given a command at Bannockburn and had no influence on the outcome of the battle, though his rearguard action ensured that the King escaped the disaster.

Gilbert de Clare, Earl of Gloucester, was 23 years of age and a nephew of Edward II, who appointed him joint commander of the vanguard along with the Earl of Hereford, which inevitably led to dispute and division in the leadership. He was very rich, probably arrogant and brought a large following with him in 1314 at his own expense, though probably not the 500 men credited to him by Barbour. Gloucester was eager for action and military distinction. He had a horse

Aymer de Valence, Earl of Pembroke, from his tomb in Westminster Abbey. Pembroke was the only English commander to emerge from the defeat at Bannockburn with any credit. He conducted a rearguard action that ensured the King's escape from the battlefield and his eventual embarkation at Dunbar. (author's drawing, after Stothard)

Sir Robert Clifford at the battle of Bannockburn. (model by the author)

Humphrey de Bohun Earl of Hereford   *Henry de Bohun*   *Gilbert de Bohun*   *Gilbert de Clare Earl of Gloucester*

killed under him on the first day of battle and, with the impetuousness of youth, rode on to the spears of the Scots and was killed the following day. He was the most important of the English casualties at Bannockburn, and his death was lamented by Robert the Bruce not only because of the loss of his huge ransom but also because he was his brother-in-law, as both had married daughters of Richard de Burgh, Earl of Ulster. He seems to have had fine notions of chivalry but none of battlefield command other than to lead recklessly from the front.

Humphrey de Bohun, Earl of Hereford, brother-in-law of the King and hereditary Constable of England, was in his early 30s at the time of Bannockburn. He had been one of the leaders of the opposition to Edward II but had been pardoned for his part in the death of Gaveston. As a youth he had fought alongside his father at the battle of Falkirk in 1298, and he was among the besiegers of Caerlaverock Castle in 1300 when he was described as 'a young man, rich and elegant'. He delighted in martial skills and jousted against Gaveston at the Wallingford tournament of 1307. As a reward for his services in Scotland, Edward I granted him Robert Bruce's castle of Lochmaben and the lands of the lordship of Annandale in 1306. De Bohun had served alongside Robert Clifford and Henry Beaumont in the north, which must have contributed to his experience of the realities of warfare. He was given joint command of the English vanguard with Gloucester before the battle of Bannockburn.

Robert d'Umfraville was a powerful Northumbrian baron and Earl of Angus, though in name alone, as the lands to which he aspired in Scotland

were divided amongst King Robert's followers. **Ingram d'Umfraville**, was Robert's cousin. He was an Anglo-Scot who had held high office in Scotland but since 1308 he had been in the service of the English. His experience should have been invaluable to Edward at Bannockburn, however, his advice regarding the Scots was rejected.

Robert Clifford was an experienced commander from the Border country who had fought at the battle of Falkirk in 1298. Clifford served both Edward II and his father before him throughout the Scottish Wars until his death at **19**

Sir Marmaduke de Thweng of Kilton Castle in Cleveland surrendered to Robert Bruce in person after the battle of Bannockburn and was generously released without ransom. (author's drawing)

The second Great Seal of King Robert I of 1316 was designed on the Continent and shows the King armed in a conventional manner. (author's drawing)

Bannockburn at the age of 40. He and Henry Beaumont led the cavalry force that clashed with Randolph's pikemen on 23 June. Apart from the Earl of Gloucester, he was the most prominent name among those killed at Bannockburn.

Henry Beaumont, a French adventurer with connections to the French Royal Family, had good reason to support Edward II in the Bannockburn campaign, for victory would have earned him a rich Scottish earldom. Beaumont's long military career extended from the battle of Falkirk in 1298, where he fought as a youth, into the 1330s, when his tactical skill brought the Scots to disaster at Dupplin Moor and contributed to Edward III's victory at Halidon Hill. It was said of him that he sought fame 'through the exercise of arms and warlike events, where danger threatened, none was more constant'.

The King's new favourite, **Hugh Despencer** the younger, was replacing the murdered Piers Gaveston in Edward's affections at this time and was at his side at Bannockburn. He had been promised the lands of the Earl of Moray, and he had brought with him the strongest retinue of knights and men-at-arms after those of the Earls of Pembroke and Gloucester to help him take them.

There were numerous veterans of Edward I's Welsh and Scottish campaigns at Bannockburn, with a wealth of military experience between them, though they ultimately failed to influence the outcome of the battle. The famous Yorkshire knight, **Marmaduke de Thweng**, who had distinguished himself at Stirling Bridge in 1297 was there, as was tough old **Thomas Berkley,** who fought as a youth at Evesham as long ago as 1265 and was said to have seen service nearly every year in the following half-century. His retinue included his soldier son Maurice and his two grandsons.

Edward II seems to have had a special regard for **Giles d'Argentan**, a formidable fighter and 'one of the three best knights in Christendom', who embodied the romantic spirit of the knight errant. Edward wrote repeatedly to the Byzantine Emperor in 1313 to secure his release from imprisonment in Salonica in time to accompany his Scottish expedition. Giles was at the King's side along with Pembroke throughout the battle, the *Scalacronica* gives him the following speech as he led the King away from the unfolding disaster: 'Sire, your rein was committed to me; you are now in safety; there is your castle where your person may be safe. I am not accustomed to fly, nor am I going to begin now. I commend you to God!' Then setting spurs to his horse he returned to the melee where he was killed. Argentan died heroically, but this kind of individual gesture did not win battles; the heroic spirit was undoubtedly essential in battle but needed to be tempered by effective leadership.

THE SCOTTISH COMMANDERS

Robert Bruce 1273–1329; Robert I, King of Scots 1306–29

Robert Bruce was born in the castle of Turnberry in Ayrshire in 1273. On the death of his father in 1304 he became the 7th Lord of Annandale in succession to be named Robert Bruce. His upbringing from an early age was as a member of the Anglo-Scottish military elite. His reputation as a brave and skilful fighter was formidable, and he was

LEFT **Flanking a highlander's spiked targe are the shields of James Douglas and Angus Og MacDonald. (author's model)**

Monumental effigy of a West Highland chief from the island of Iona. Angus Og would have been armed and equipped in this manner; Barbour confirms his presence at Bannockburn and calls him 'Syre Angus of Ile'.

rated as one of the 'three best knights in Christendom', the others being the Emperor Henry VII and Sir Giles d'Argentan.

Bruce's strategy for the recovery and liberation of Scotland with the limited forces at his disposal can hardly be faulted. He did not take unnecessary risks and avoided battle when the odds were stacked too greatly against him, preferring instead a Fabian strategy. It has been said that Bruce's experience as a commander before Bannockburn was limited to irregular or partisan warfare. There is no doubt that he excelled in this field, for under his tutelage his tiny force became successful and feared guerrilla fighters, constantly moving, using lightning raids, ambush and night attack to strike terror amongst their enemies. In a number of actions, at Glen Trool, Loudon Hill, at the Hill of Barra and at the Pass of Brander, Bruce, with determined men that he had carefully welded into a fighting force, displayed a mastery of battlefield tactics. These were admittedly actions fought on a small scale, with no more than 1,000 men under his command, yet when events moved on to a broader canvas in 1314, Bruce would show that the basic tenets of command on the battlefield remained the same and his grasp of them equally sound.

Bruce's commanders at Bannockburn had fought alongside him from the early days of his struggle against the English. **James 'the Black' Douglas**, later the 'Good' Sir James, joined Bruce at the age of 18 after his father, Sir William Douglas, an implacable opponent of the English, was murdered in the Tower of London. The Douglas lands were forfeit and were given to Sir Robert Clifford. As a guerrilla leader, Douglas soon gained a fearsome reputation for his merciless slaughter of the English garrisons of the south-west of Scotland. Yet his youthful boldness was tempered by cunning, for it was his initiative that led to the surprise and capture of mighty Roxburgh Castle. It has been suggested that his importance before Bannockburn has been overestimated and that his role during the battle has been exaggerated. On the first day of battle he commanded a cavalry detachment and carried out a reconnaissance role. Though Barbour suggests that Douglas had command of a fourth Scottish division, it is more likely that on the following day he dismounted his men and led them as a sub-division of a schiltron of pikemen. Later in the day he remounted the remnants of his force and led the pursuit of Edward II.

King Robert's only surviving brother in 1314, **Edward Bruce**, has been accused of boldness bordering on the foolhardy, yet his conduct at Bannockburn, under the leadership of his brother, was that of a reliable subordinate commander. He commanded one of the three divisions or schiltrons of pikemen during the battle. In 1318, left to his own devices, his brief tenure of the title 'King of Ireland' ended when he was defeated and killed at Dundalk in County Louth.

Thomas Randolph was the nephew of Robert Bruce and one of his earliest adherents. He was captured by the English and served them until 1309 when he rejoined Bruce. His subsequent loyalty and service was rewarded in 1312 with the great northern earldom of Moray. He commanded one of the three Scottish schiltrons at Bannockburn.

Sir Robert Keith was an Anglo-Scot from Lothian who joined Bruce in 1308. He was rather older than the other commanders and, as hereditary Marshal of Scotland, was a man of high social rank. Barbour gives him command of an armoured cavalry force of 500 men at Bannockburn, but it is more likely that, on the second day of battle, along with other Scottish knights of his station, he fought dismounted; his men forming a sub-division of a schiltron.

Bruce had formed a strong bond with his experienced commanders and shared a unity of purpose with them. In marked contrast, almost the first we hear of the English leadership is of the discord between Gloucester and Hereford over a matter of personal prestige.

'Robert the Bruce, King of Scots', sculpted by Charles Pilkington Jackson and erected on the site of the Borestone at Bannockburn in 1965. A cast of Bruce's skull, which was uncovered in Dunfermline Abbey in 1819, was used by the sculptor to help reconstruct his appearance.

OPPOSING ARMIES

THE ENGLISH ARMY OF 1314

Sir William Fitzralph, from his monumental brass in Pebmarsh Church, Essex c.1320. The Fitzralph brass is probably the best contemporary evidence of the armour that was worn by well-equipped knights at Bannockburn. Armour was in transition at this time and, although plate defences for most parts of the body had been devised, a full harness of mail is still worn. A cuirass of *cuir-bouilli* or metal plates was worn beneath the surcoat. A helm or visored bascinet was worn over the mail aventail.

Edward II's cavalry included both feudal and paid contingents, as well as the mounted troops of his household. His infantry were either spearmen or archers but it is not clear in what proportion. A typical Edwardian army was organised into three divisions or 'battles'. The constable, who was responsible for the organisation and conduct of the army, customarily commanded the vanguard or fore-battle. At Bannockburn the constable was the Earl of Hereford, though the honour was confused by Edward II's appointment of Gloucester as joint commander of the vanguard. The main-battle was by custom commanded by the king if he was present, so we can be sure that Edward II was with the centre division and that he would have had his household troops under his seneschal, Sir Edmund Mauley, with him. As to the reserve or rear-battle, there is no direct evidence about the leadership of this formation at Bannockburn. We know that the English army approached Stirling in good order with the vanguard appropriately leading the advance but, after their setbacks of the first day's fighting, confusion rather than order seems to have been the keyword. Barbour tells us that the English King divided his men into ten divisions and appointed men who were known to be good commanders to each. If Edward had about 10,000 infantry, as seems likely, then this arrangement would seem probable.

The English Cavalry

The feudal system allowed the king to demand that his tenants-in-chief provide him with a quota of horsemen who were to serve for 40 days, though by Edward II's time the custom was that the barons brought fewer men who served longer. In 1310 the Earl of Pembroke was summoned to the muster at Berwick and, though he refused to attend personally, he acknowledged that he owed the King the service of five knights; an obligation he would fulfil by providing one knight and eight 'servientes' or men-at-arms, with ten 'barded' horses. From this it follows that the horse and equipment of a man-at-arms cost only half that of a knight. The 1310 muster at Berwick produced only 37 knights and 472 men-at-arms as the obstructive barons sent the lowest possible number of inferior quality horsemen. Similarly, in 1314 the Earl of Lancaster and his faction ignored Edward II's summons and sent only a minimum quota of horsemen to the muster at Berwick.

The King also raised horsemen from those whose property was valued at £20, a 'knight's fee', or over, which obliged them to serve as a knight or to provide a substitute; these horsemen had to be paid for their service. In theory at least there were over 5,000 knights available for service, but men

A lighter form of horse armour; the vulnerable fore parts of the horse are protected by a defence of *cuir-bouilli* with domed metal reinforcements. (redrawn by the author from a mid-14th-century illustration)

A rare depiction of an armoured horse from the seal of William Montague, Earl of Salisbury. The seal is of the 1330s but similar mail horse coverings were in use at the time of Bannockburn. A powerful beast would have been needed to carry a full-mail trapper in addition to an armoured rider. (author's drawing)

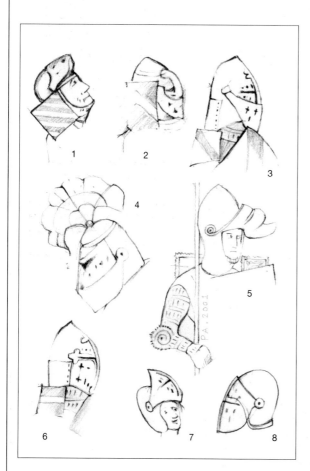

Early 14th century helmets and bascinets. 1. Visored bascinet. 2–4. Helms with articulated lower gorget plates. 5. Visored bascinet. 6. Typical early 14th-century helm with pointed top. 7–8. Visored bascinet and reconstruction. (author's drawing)

The sculpture on the canopy of the tomb of Aymer de Valence in Westminster Abbey shows not only an early visored bascinet but also this curious chapel-de-fer style helmet, suggesting a far greater variety of equipment existed than the standardised monuments of the period lead us to believe.

were not always eager to take up knighthood and the King regularly had to bring pressure to bear on reticent warriors, 'who ought to be knights and are not'. A valuable source of information from Edward I's time is the series of Horse-Lists, that record the names of each horseman in the King's pay together with the value and a description of his horse, so that the owner could be reimbursed if the animal was killed in the King's service. These lists tell us that at the battle of Falkirk in 1298, Edward I's paid cavalry together with his household contingent numbered 1,300. The feudal levy would have added between 500 and 1,000 men, which would give the King a cavalry force of around 2,300 men at the most. The well-informed Monk of Malmesbury tells us in the *Vita Edwardi Secundi*, that for the Bannockburn campaign, 'the cavalry numbered more than two thousand'; a sober estimate in an age noted for wild exaggeration in the matter of numbers. Both the knights and men-at-arms of this formidable striking force were heavy armoured cavalry mounted on what were referred to as 'barded' or 'covered' horses, by which presumably a protective covering is meant. There is less direct surviving evidence for the Bannockburn campaign than for that of Falkirk, as most of the documentation that would have allowed us to form an idea of the true numbers of the English army was lost, probably along with the privy seal, during the rout that followed the battle. However the 'protections', listed in the Scotch Roll for 1314, by which the King undertook to protect the lands and goods of men who were away in his service, cover some 890 mounted men, knights, esquires and men-at-arms, so we know the minimum number that should have set out for Berwick. The numbers suggest a force that may have equalled that fielded by Edward I at Falkirk.

The English Infantry

The foot levies of southern England were not summoned for service in Scottish campaigns, only the northern and Midland counties and Wales were called upon. On 24 March 1314, Edward II summoned from these areas 21,540 foot – a formidable array had it materialised – who were to muster at Wark-on-Tweed by 10 June. Evidence from previous campaigns, however, suggests that the system of raising troops would at best provide Edward with just over half the number called for and a proportion of those would desert at the first opportunity. A writ of 9 March 1314 summoning 4,500 archers from five northern counties, 'with bows and arrows and other competent arms', indicates that a strong force of well-equipped bowmen was envisaged. This order was superseded by a more extensive call-out, but unfortunately these later writs are not specific, they simply demand foot soldiers, making it difficult to assess the ratio of bowmen to spearmen in the army. As late as 29 May, Edward wrote urgently to his commissioners of array '… We have ordered the men to be ready at a date already past … you are to exasperate and hurry up and compel the men to come.' Edward's wording suggests difficulties in raising infantry, a situation that would inevitably result in unwilling and poor quality recruits arriving at Berwick too late to be made into a cohesive and effective fighting force.

Archers

The regions from which the infantry was assembled for the Bannockburn campaign, the north of England, the Midland counties and Wales were all areas famed for the prowess of their longbowmen. When the writs of

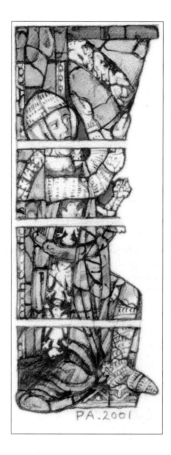

Sir Robert Mauley, who was captured at Bannockburn, 'Or, on a bend sable 3 eagles displayed argent'. The armour is conventional; all mail, apart from the plate poleyns or knee cops. (author's drawing from the Mauley Window in York Minster)

There was a widespread trade in armour throughout Europe and styles were similar from one country to another in the early 14th century. Most of the knightly armour at Bannockburn would have been made on the continent. There are many similarities between the armour of the Bavarian knight Konrad von Heideck c.1310 and that of English effigies of the same date. (Photo Hans Trauner)

9 March 1314 are compared to those that superseded them on 27 May, it will be seen that the 2,000 archers requested from Yorkshire becomes 4,000 unspecified foot soldiers. The 1,000 Nottinghamshire and Derbyshire archers demanded becomes 2,000 foot, and though the other figures do not bear out my assumption quite as neatly, it might be assumed that the ratio of longbowmen to spearmen was envisaged as being roughly equal. Roger Mortimer was commanded to raise 3,000 foot in Wales for the campaign. The chronicler Gerald of Wales noted that there was a characteristic difference between Welshmen; those of the north fought as spearmen while the men of the south were longbowmen. So it is probable that of the 3,000 foot raised by Roger Mortimer in Wales, the 1,000 men that he raised in South Wales were longbowmen and the 2,000 men raised in North Wales were spearmen.

The town of Bristol was called upon for 100 crossbowmen and archers, so it seems that the towns were to furnish a proportion of crossbowmen, but there is no telling what proportion of crossbowmen to longbowmen was expected. As the crossbow was an expensive weapon to manufacture it is likely that only contingents from the prosperous towns were armed with them, so the overall numbers with the army would be relatively small. The crossbow in use at this date was spanned with the help of a belt-hook or goat's-foot lever and, though it did not have the rate of fire of a longbow, it was by no means as cumbersome and slow a weapon as the steel-bowed, windlass crossbows that came into use later in the 14th century.

Foreign Contingents and Mercenaries

John Barbour relates that there were French knights, Gascons, Dutch, Bretons and men from Poitou, Aquitaine and Bayonne in the English army, and he tells of the many Scots who fought for Edward II at Bannockburn. Barbour mentions German knights too and Friar Baston confirms this but says that only four German knights came though they served 'gratis'. The hiring of foreign troops was normally very expensive. Barbour mistakenly thought that the Count of Hainault was at Bannockburn; in fact he and his men served against the Scots in 1326 and 1327 when the bill for their services, which resulted in practically nothing, came to an astonishing £55,000! It is probable that Edward's foreign contingents were mentioned by Barbour because of their exotic nature rather than their large numbers. Twenty-five Irish chiefs were summoned to serve in the 1314 campaign as well as a number of Anglo-Irish knights but we don't know how many of these turned out. Richard de Burgh, the Red Earl of Ulster, was with Edward II at Newminster Abbey in Northumberland on 29 May and would have had some Irish troops with him.

Tactics

The Welsh and Scottish Wars provide several examples of the inability of unsupported cavalry to break steady formations of pikemen. At the battle of Builth in 1282, Walter of Hemingburgh tells us that the Welsh were cut down and put to flight by the English cavalry because the archers 'were fighting by concert in between our cavalry'. Similarly, at Maes Madoc in 1295, the Earl of Warwick, with a picked force of cavalry and archers, confronted the spearmen of North Wales who, 'rested the butts of their spears on the ground and presenting the points when the English horse charged held them off. But the earl posted a crossbowman between each pair of horsemen, or an archer for the number of crossbows was very small, and when many of the spearmen had been brought down by bolts, the horse charged again and defeated them with great slaughter.' The chronicler Nicholas Trevet's account is clear; it is the combination of horsemen and archers that proves irresistible, not the cavalry alone. Heminburgh revealed that, at the battle of Falkirk in 1298, Edward I's ill-disciplined cavalry charged the Scottish spearmen, 'who were like a thick wood, and could not force their way in because of the number of spears … But our foot shot at them with arrows and some with stones which lay there in plenty. So many were slain and the front ranks pushed back on the rear ranks in confusion, and then our horse broke in and routed them.' Aymer de Valence, Robert Clifford, Henry Beaumont, Humphrey de Bohun and Giles d'Argentan were all in the thick of the fighting at Falkirk, yet not one of them seems to have profited by the experience, least of all Clifford and Beaumont, who conspicuously led their unsupported squadrons of horse to bloody defeat against Moray's spearmen.

Edward II's army was not the hand-picked, disciplined force that Warwick so ably led at Maes Madoc. The army of Bannockburn was a large, unwieldy and amorphous assemblage of disparate elements led by a king who was no soldier. The tactical problem of combining horse and foot implied some bridging of the social gap that existed between the two, and at Bannockburn the gap loomed large. The feckless leadership allowed the arrogant and over confident knighthood to wilfully disregard their social inferiors on foot and ride unsupported to disaster. The infantry were of course aware that if the horse were decisively repulsed, then all were repulsed, and they would be left to shift for themselves, mere fodder for the grim reaper. Only when the two elements were combined would they stand firm; thus at Bannockburn, when the foot saw the defeat of the cavalry, they knew it was a losing game and their first thought was of flight.

THE SCOTTISH ARMY OF 1314

Scotland, being a small and impoverished nation, could never field a force of mounted men to rival the armoured chivalry of England. The Scots were essentially infantry, and they relied on their schiltrons of spearmen to bear the brunt of the fighting with support from archers and a small light cavalry force. The population of Scotland in the early 14th century was barely a fifth of England's and Bruce could not draw upon the whole country as many still supported the English or, particularly in Lothian where they were exposed to retaliation, remained prudently neutral. Nevertheless, the army that Bruce assembled outside Stirling in the summer of 1314 was a formidable fighting force; well trained and led, and motivated by a unity of purpose that was lacking in the English, for the Scots were defending their homes and independence. Bruce put his faith not in numbers but in men of spirit, and he told any who were weak of courage to depart in good time as he wanted only men who would 'wyn all or die with honour'.

The Scottish National Flag and Arms, Azure a saltire argent, are of great antiquity and it is probable that the Scottish infantry wore this badge from an early date.

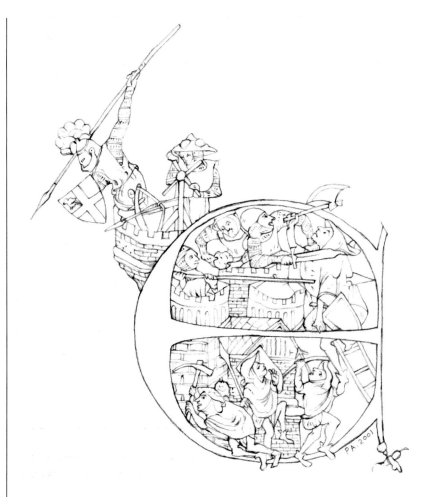

The Scottish army was organised conventionally into three divisions. The vanguard was commanded by Thomas Randolph, whose men were drawn from his own earldom of Moray, from the far north and from Inverness and the towns of the north-east. The centre or main-battle was not commanded by the King but entrusted to Edward Bruce, who had with him the men of Buchan, Mar, Angus, the Mearns, Menteith, Strathearn, Lennox and a contingent from Galloway. King Robert commanded the reserve or rear-battle, which was formed by his own men of Carrick together with the lowlanders of southern Scotland, contingents from the highland clans and Angus Og MacDonald's men from Argyll and the Western Isles.

The initial letter from the Carlisle Charter of 1316 shows the siege of Carlisle that took place the previous year. The four Scottish soldiers attacking the town wear no body armour but appear to have some form of protective headgear. They may be highlanders wearing plaids with a fold drawn over the head against the weather, which was notably bad in 1315. The axeman on the ladder carries a triangular shield as does the spearman below. The miner with a pickaxe has just been hit by a rock dropped from above and a Scottish archer is about to let fly at this well-armed assailant. The knight in the turret is Sir Andrew Harcla, who organised the successful defence of Carlisle. (author's drawing)

English sources for the battle state that there were a conventional three Scottish infantry divisions at Bannockburn, but Barbour adds a fourth, commanded by James Douglas and the youthful High Steward of Scotland. Barbour also tells us that Robert Bruce sent James Douglas and the Marshal, Sir Robert Keith, to reconnoitre the approach of the English army before the battle: 'They mounted and rode forth, having well-horsed men with them'. At the end of the battle when Edward II fled defeated, Douglas with his small mounted force was sent in pursuit, but, 'he had far too few horse, having fewer than sixty in his force.' It seems from this that not only Sir Robert Keith but also James Douglas commanded bodies of mounted troops at Bannockburn, though they may have dismounted on the second day of fighting and fought on foot alongside the pikemen. If Douglas had had an independent infantry command it is unlikely that Bruce would twice have detached him from this important role to take off with the cavalry.

John Barbour wrote his epic poem 'The Bruce' in 1376 during the reign of the first Stewart King, Robert II, and he may well have enhanced the role of the young High Steward, his ancestor, at Bannockburn to humour the King. James Douglas was not as important a figure before 1314 as popular imagination might believe; he was not even a knight until Bruce conferred the accolade on the night of 23/24 June. He was, however, as much the hero of Barbour's epic tale as the Bruce himself so his importance before the battle may also have been overstated. It is

Scottish weapons from medieval West Highland monuments.
1. Spear.
2–7. Long-handled fighting axes.
8. Targe.
9. Ballock dagger.
10. Quiver, probably for crossbow bolts.
(redrawn by the author after RCAHMS)

improbable that the relatively lowly Douglas would have been given command of an infantry division in company with Edward Bruce, the Earl of Moray and the King himself.

The Scottish Schiltron
Schiltrum or *schiltron*, meaning a shield wall, has been habitually used to describe formations, generally taken to be circles or hollow rings of Scottish pikemen because the word occurs in the chronicler Guisborough's account of the battle of Falkirk. Barbour does not call the Scottish infantry formations at Bannockburn schiltrums but does use the word to describe the disordered English; 'for all their divisions were together in a schiltrum', by which he means crowded together, in a bunch, without formation. Sir Thomas Grey describes the Scots advance at Bannockburn as 'all aligned in schiltron', or aligned in close order. Other than troops in close order, no particular formation, weapon or tactic is implied by the use of the word schiltron.

The Scottish Infantry
The backbone of the Scottish army was its formations of pikemen, formed six ranks deep and presenting an impenetrable barrier bristling with iron-tipped pikes to the heavily armoured English cavalry. Impenetrable, yet static and thus vulnerable to troops armed with missile weapons. Sir Thomas Grey tells us that 'the Scots had taken a lesson from the Flemings, who before that had at Courtrai defeated on foot the power of France'. No doubt Bruce knew about Courtrai, but he

Scottish single-handed swords from medieval West Highland monuments.
1–5. The lobated pommels are typical of Scottish swords of the 14th century and show their Viking derivation. No examples of this type of weapon have survived.
6–7. Swords of Scottish medieval type with typical depressed quillions and disc pommel. The double-handed 'claymore' did not come into use in Scotland until around 1500.
(redrawn by the author after RCAHMS)

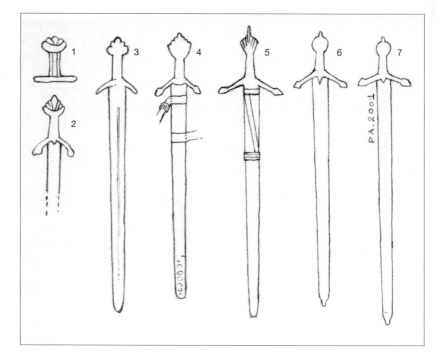

would also have been acutely aware of the defeat inflicted by the English on Wallace's pikemen at Falkirk. Whatever lessons he drew from the past, Bruce realised that the long Scottish pikes were a heavy and cumbersome weapon and were only effective if the men were well organised and trained. He knew that it was not enough for the pikemen to stand fast against a charge of cavalry; his formations had to be able to advance and change direction if they were to play a decisive role. The behaviour of Moray's pikemen on 23 June illustrates not only their manoeuvrability, when his force quickly took the open field to block Clifford's way to Stirling Castle, but also displays their training as the rear ranks faced about to confront the enveloping horsemen. We should not imagine, however, that a medieval Scottish army exercised with the precision of Prussian Guardsmen; at best it would have displayed a rather ragged uniformity of purpose.

We are afforded a glimpse of some of the arms and equipment of the Scottish infantry by a decree made by the Scottish Parliament at Scone in 1318, when it was decided that men worth £10 in goods were to have a sword, plate gloves and an iron hat or bascinet, their armour was to be either a padded and quilted *akheton* or a mail shirt or *haubergeon*. A second category of men worth goods to the value of a cow were to be armed with a spear or bow. Though no armour is mentioned, this was the minimum equipment they were required to bring to the muster. Clearly archers formed part of the Scottish army, but we cannot tell from the above what ratio of spearmen to bowmen was intended. The lowland infantry, who formed the bulk of Scottish armies, would not have looked much different to their English counterparts. There is no mention of a shield or targe; the infantry were pikemen and needed both hands to handle the unwieldy weapon, there was no place for shields in the densely packed ranks of the Scots. 'Blackmail' levied from the northern counties of England financed much of Bruce's war effort, allowing him

30

to equip his fighting men with well-made armour and weapons purchased from the Low Countries and the Hanseatic towns.

There were men from Argyll, Kintyre and the Western Isles at Bannockburn and the traditions of a score of highland clans assert their presence there too. The highlanders fought in King Robert's division, and it is probable that, however outlandish their dress, they fought like the lowlanders as pikemen or archers. We can't be certain how King Robert trained his army but there can be little doubt that the men were drilled in small units until these could be integrated into larger ones. The events of the two days' fighting show an efficient chain of command holding the structure together and enabling Bruce to impose his will on his army.

Scottish Archers

The Scots had been conspicuously deficient in archers before King Robert's day, and there is evidence that he altered feudal obligations of knight service into archer service to remedy this. An instance of this change is provided by the barony of Manor in Tweeddale which formed one knight's fee and was to provide, instead of a knight, ten archers. Bruce obviously knew the danger posed by the English longbowmen and intended to counter the threat with a sizeable force of his own. Archers were drawn from the Borders and southern Scotland in the main, though the bow was in use in the highlands too. Scottish archers were equipped with the longbow, the yew staves probably being imported via the Hanseatic ports. A later, though unmistakable, longbow is illustrated on a West Highland grave-slab at Arisaig. There is no reason to suppose that the Scots used a shorter, less powerful bow than their English and Welsh counterparts; their inferiority lay in numbers rather than in a lack of longbows.

Scottish Axemen

The Lochaber axe was a favoured weapon of the highlanders and a similar polearm, the Jedart axe, was used with terrible effect in the lowlands. It is probable that a proportion of Scots at Bannockburn fought with these weapons, possibly intermingled in groups with the pikemen. Barbour mentions fighters who 'shoot out of their formation, stab horses … and bring men down'. Clearly these men were not armed with the unwieldy pike but with swords, daggers, axes and polearms, weapons more suited to close-quarter fighting.

The Scottish Cavalry

The small Scottish cavalry force under the hereditary Marshal, Sir Robert Keith, probably numbered less than the 500 men attributed to it by Barbour. It is unlikely that there were many heavily armoured knights among them. Their role, in contrast to the English heavy horse, was not that of a main striking force, nor were they intended to counter this threat. Their role was that of light cavalry, and as such they reconnoitred the approaching English army and warned Bruce of the strength of the enemy.

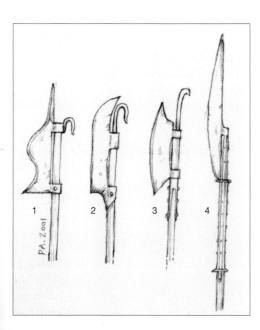

Scottish medieval polearms, 1–4. Jedburgh or Jedart axes. It is probable that neither the terms 'Jedburgh axe' nor 'Lochaber axe' inferred a specific shape of blade but meant roughly a fighting bill. The terms 'Jedburgh' or 'Lochaber' being attached to them because of their habitual use by the fighting men of these areas. (author's drawing)

1   2   3   4

PA.2001

They did not have the capability to face the English cavalry and may in fact have dismounted to fight alongside the pikemen on foot on the second day of battle. Contemporary sources all agree that the Scots fought on foot at Bannockburn and make no mention of Scottish cavalry and this has been taken as evidence to deny their existence. Yet John Barbour's account of the mounted reconnaissance force led by Douglas and Keith is entirely credible, as is the story of the inability of Douglas at the end of the battle to mount enough men for an effective pursuit of the English King. Only Barbour's tale of the Scottish cavalry charge that resulted in the rout of the English archers is questionable. Could so small a force of light cavalry have ridden down a formation of archers that was large enough to pose a threat to the advance of the Scottish infantry? It may be that Barbour invented the incident to account for what seemed to him the inexplicable failure of the feared bowmen to influence the battle. Yet he is far too convincing and well informed a writer for us to dismiss the details in his account simply because the English sources, admittedly earlier, fail to mention them.

Recently there has been speculation about the presence of Templar knights at Bannockburn. The Order had ceased to exist by 1312 when it was officially suppressed by the Pope. The French disposed of the Grand Master of the Temple and 45 Templar knights by burning them in Paris in 1314. In England the Templars were dispossessed with more decorum and the Master of the Temple was simply pensioned off. In Scotland, as early as October 1309, John de Segrave, the King's lieutenant, was ordered to round up Templars still at large in that country. It is quite possible that former Scottish Templars fought in the ranks of King Robert's army, but they would not have done so under the Templars' famous 'Beauseant' banner.

OPPOSING PLANS

ENGLISH PLANS

The number of men that Edward II summoned to serve in 1314 and the scale of the preparations he put in train for his overdue expedition against the Scots suggest that this was a full-scale invasion aimed at nothing short of the total subjugation of the Scots. The compact between Philip Moubray and Edward Bruce merely added an urgency to the invasion preparations and introduced a deadline for Edward's appearance before Stirling Castle. The immensely strong castle, perched on its rock dominating the town and the bridge over the River Forth, had been in English hands since Edward I took it in 1304. Any invasion of Scotland had to take account of its strategic position in the waist of Scotland at the first bridging point of the River Forth, guarding the narrow neck of land between the Firths of Forth and Clyde; its possession was the key to the north of Scotland.

The logistical planning of the campaign was left to capable officers, and the English army was well supplied by the commissariat on their well-ordered march north. King Edward had good intelligence reports of the preparations of the Scots before Stirling, he was not short of experienced advisors and appears to have been aware of the value of infantry in the difficult terrain in Scotland. Yet there is no evidence from events to show that Edward had any battle plan at all in mind at Bannockburn, nor did he display a control of his army that might have enabled him to have put a plan in motion. If the King had ever learned the lessons of the Welsh Wars and the battle of Falkirk, they were forgotten; there was no thought of combining infantry and cavalry in a planned attack. The headstrong knights were allowed to assert their independence by artlessly attempting to bludgeon their way through the ranks of the Scots. Edward's assumption that the Scots would simply melt away before him was proved wrong by their aggressive resistance, and by the end of the first day's fighting whatever plans the hapless King may have had lay in ruin. He lost control of events and the initiative passed to the Scots.

SCOTTISH PLANS

Robert Bruce knew that Edward II's army could be expected before Stirling Castle by Midsummer Day of 1314. Bruce's small, well-tried army became the nucleus of the larger army that he gathered in the Torwood in response to this threat. It is not certain that Bruce intended to fight a battle, though he clearly meant to harass the enemy in the woods through which the road to Stirling from the south ran, and may well have dug a series of 'pottes' or traps to impede the advance of the

English cavalry. He was above all a cautious commander and throughout his career he displayed a reluctance to risk all on the uncertain outcome of a battle when the odds were against him, and he knew from his reconnaissance force that the English were advancing in great strength. During Edward II's previous invasion of Scotland in 1310, Bruce's response had been to withdraw into the interior leaving the land burnt and bare of food and forage until winter's cold and rain and the escalating cost of supplying and paying a large army in the field forced the English to withdraw. Bruce's dispositions in the New Park suggest that he had this course of action in mind. Defeat outside Stirling would have been ruinous for his cause and he must have pondered on the fate of Wallace and the plight of Scotland after the defeat at Falkirk.

But there were disadvantages in a Fabian strategy. Stirling would be relieved and the door to the north and the vital port of Perth would be open. Edward might gain far more than a toehold on the country before the onset of winter. It was high summer and the ranks of the Scots army were swollen with fresh fighting men eager for battle, so Bruce took care that his dispositions allowed him not only to withdraw safely but also to face about and fight if a favourable opportunity presented itself.

THE CAMPAIGN

THE SIEGE OF STIRLING CASTLE

In October 1313 a hollow accommodation had been patched up between Edward II and the Earl of Lancaster and his faction who, in turn for a humble apology for their part in Gaveston's murder, were granted a pardon. The political situation was now stable enough for Edward to turn his attention to the desperate situation in Scotland and in November a campaign was decided on, prompted by further events in the north. In October 1313, at an assembly in Dundee, Robert Bruce had given those Scots who had not yet come into his peace a year to swear fealty to him or lose their lands. At about the same time, the hard-pressed Anglo-Scots of Lothian appealed to Edward II for protection and he, perhaps alarmed by King Robert's threat, promised to bring an army to Scotland by midsummer the following year. Early in 1314 the English position further deteriorated when James Douglas surprised and captured the important castle of Roxburgh and, not to be outdone by Douglas's bold exploit, Thomas Randolph took Edinburgh Castle by escalade in a daring night attack. Outside Lothian only the great strongholds of Bothwell and Stirling remained in English hands. Walter Gilbertson, the castellan of Bothwell, was isolated and presented no immediate threat so, after the fall of Edinburgh, King Robert turned his attention to the reduction of mighty Stirling Castle, the guardian of the gateway between the north and south of the realm. Edward Bruce was

The earliest extant drawing of Stirling Castle shows a quite different structure to the building we see today. (author's drawing from an early 15th-century illustration)

The main gateway to Stirling Castle, the buildings of the present castle date mostly from the 15th and 16th centuries. (photo Peter Ryder)

entrusted by his brother with the siege of Stirling, but without siege engines there was little he could do except blockade the castle and wait. Philip Moubray, the beleaguered governor, realised that the fall of Stirling was but a matter of time and came to an agreement with Edward that if he was not relieved by 24 June he would surrender the castle. Such chivalrous arrangements were quite common in those days and allowed the protagonists relief from the realities of siege warfare. On 27 May Edward II, who was already on his way north to the muster of his army at Berwick, was informed of the agreement, which put him under pressure to relieve Stirling by this deadline. He would have been alerted by the messenger to the unfavourable terrain south of the castle and the fact that the Scots army was in a strong position there. King Robert was not pleased with his brother's chivalrous gesture towards Moubray, he realised that the deadline would spur the English to action and that the time scale allowed that the castle might well be relieved. Only a pitched battle would prevent it, and he had no wish to be committed to any course of action that could destroy what he had achieved so far.

Early in March 1314 Edward II began to issue a stream of orders that put in train the gathering of men and supplies for the invasion of Scotland. Money to finance the campaign had been raised by a loan from the Papacy, secured against income from Edward's lands in France. Aymer de Valence, Earl of Pembroke, was appointed as the King's lieutenant in Scotland. The date set for the muster was 10 June and from his headquarters in Berwick, Pembroke enrolled and organised the troops gathering along the Tweed in the shadow of the great Border fortresses of Norham and Wark.

An immense amount of food and equipment was brought north by sea and, as the English had no secure supply bases left in Scotland, a huge wagon train was assembled to cart the army's supplies overland. Everything needed for the campaign had to be stockpiled and transported, as King Robert would see that there was little of use left in the path of the invasion. By 29 May Edward II's unhurried progress north found him at Newminster Abbey in Northumberland. The machinery of government accompanied him and the output of the everyday minutiae necessary for the administration of the realm flowed unchecked throughout the campaign, thus enabling us to chart his whereabouts day by day. Though many of the clerks and scribes remained in Berwick when Edward marched into Scotland, a considerable number along with the great Privy Seal of England accompanied him. From Newminster Edward wrote to his Commissioners of Array asking them to send the infantry he had summoned urgently as 'the Scots are striving to assemble great numbers of foot in strong and marshy places, extremely hard for cavalry to penetrate, between us and our castle of Stirling'. It is evident from this that Edward had good intelligence reports and must have appreciated the need for a strong infantry force to oust the Scots from their positions in front of Stirling in the forthcoming campaign. An appeal for troops at the end of May left little time for them to reach the muster, as it would take the crossbowmen summoned from distant Bristol at least three weeks to march to Berwick. The spearmen of North Wales could have reached the muster in about 17 days but the archers of South Wales would have needed a week longer. It may have been because of a shortage of infantry that the invasion was delayed until the last moment. When he arrived at Berwick, Edward,

Stirling Castle from the south looking across the King's Park. (Nigel Kelman)

whose generosity with other people's property was limitless, encouraged his predatory followers by distributing lands and titles in Scotland in advance of his conquest.

EDWARD II MARCHES NORTH, 17–22 JUNE 1314

On 17 June English columns forded the River Tweed at Wark and Coldstream and headed on the rough tracks of the undulating Merse of Berwickshire towards the foothills of the Lammermuir Hills, an easy day's march away. Edward had considered the advantages of taking the coastal route from Berwick but had preferred the inland route, as it was passable by wheeled transport and offered a quicker and more direct route north for the army. The weather that summer was kind and did not delay the advance, in fact it seems to have had no influence on the course of the campaign at all. We have an indirect clue to the weather in 1314 from the author of the 'Annals of London' who follows his list of the casualties at Bannockburn with the information that the year following the battle was 'a year of rains'. We can infer from this that the same was not true of 1314 and that the weather that summer was fair or at least unremarkable. The Earl of Pembroke, who knew the country well, rode ahead of the army with a mounted force but met with no opposition. The Monk of Malmesbury wrote that 'Never in our time did

The mound and earthworks of Wark Castle stand high above the fords of the river Tweed. Very little masonry survives of what was once one of the most important of Border fortresses.

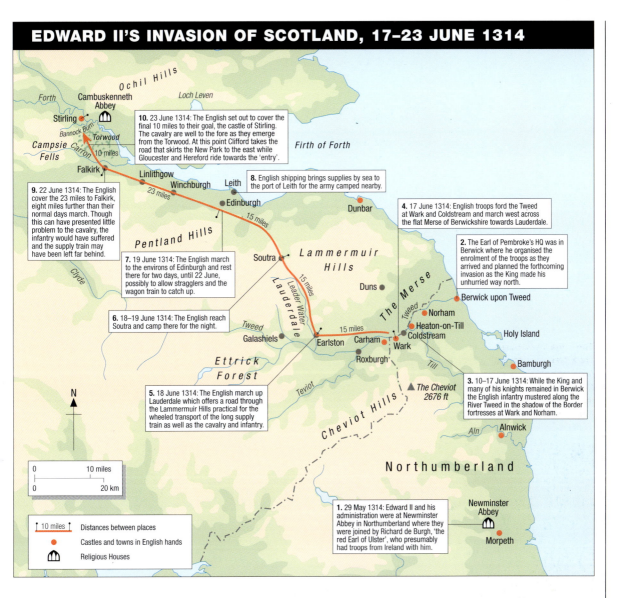

10. 23 June 1314: The English set out to cover the final 10 miles to their goal, the castle of Stirling. The cavalry are well to the fore as they emerge from the Torwood. At this point Clifford takes the road that skirts the New Park to the east while Gloucester and Hereford ride towards the 'entry'.

8. English shipping brings supplies by sea to the port of Leith for the army camped nearby.

9. 22 June 1314: The English cover the 23 miles to Falkirk, eight miles further than their normal days march. Though this can have presented little problem to the cavalry, the infantry would have suffered and the supply train may have been left far behind.

4. 17 June 1314: English troops ford the Tweed at Wark and Coldstream and march west across the flat Merse of Berwickshire towards Lauderdale.

2. The Earl of Pembroke's HQ was in Berwick where he organised the enrolment of the troops as they arrived and planned the forthcoming invasion as the King made his unhurried way north.

7. 19 June 1314: The English march to the environs of Edinburgh and rest there for two days, until 22 June, possibly to allow stragglers and the wagon train to catch up.

6. 18–19 June 1314: The English reach Soutra and camp there for the night.

5. 18 June 1314: The English march up Lauderdale which offers a road through the Lammermuir Hills practical for the wheeled transport of the long supply train as well as the cavalry and infantry.

3. 10–17 June 1314: While the King and many of his knights remained in Berwick the English infantry mustered along the River Tweed in the shadow of the Border fortresses at Wark and Norham.

1. 29 May 1314: Edward II and his administration were at Newminster Abbey in Northumberland where they were joined by Richard de Burgh, 'the red Earl of Ulster', who presumably had troops from Ireland with him.

10 miles — Distances between places

Castles and towns in English hands

Religious Houses

such an army quit England. The multitude of carts stretched out in a line would have taken up twenty leagues.'

The following day, 18 June, the army crossed the Lammermuir Hills on the line of the Roman road that wound up Lauderdale and across the moors to Soutra, where they camped for the night. The next day the English army traversed the 15 miles of undulating country that brought them to Edinburgh. Here they waited until 21 June to allow the wagon train of over 200 baggage and supply wagons, which straggled behind the long columns of horse and foot, to catch up. Edward hoped the rest day would allow much needed infantry, who had arrived late for the muster, to join them. At the nearby port of Leith, English supply ships landed stores for the troops, who would be well rested before the 35-mile march that would bring them to Stirling Castle before the 24 June deadline. By the evening of Saturday, 22 June, forward elements of the English army were in the environs of Falkirk. Less than ten miles, and Bruce's army massed south of Stirling, now lay between them and their objective.

OPPOSITE, TOP **The fords across the Tweed below Wark Castle where Edward II's army crossed into Scotland on 17 June 1314. Beyond is the flat countryside of the Merse of Berwickshire.**

OPPOSITE, BOTTOM **Norham Castle guards an important ford of the River Tweed midway between the castles of Berwick and Wark. Edward II assembled his invasion force along the line of the river in the shadow of these fortresses. (photo Peter Ryder)**

BELOW **Little remains of Berwick Castle, one of the most famous of Border strongholds. This part of the curtain wall, known as the White Wall, leads down to the Water Tower where a boom or chain crossed to the other bank of the Tweed to prevent the passage of hostile craft. (photo Peter Ryder)**

The *Vita* paints a grim picture of Edward's advance into Scotland: 'Short time was allowed for sleep, shorter for meals. Horses, horsemen and infantry, overcome by toil and want of food are not to be blamed for their failure in battle.' Yet this seems a feeble excuse as the army was apparently well supplied and marched only a steady 15 miles a day until it reached Edinburgh. By comparison the Roman Army marched about 18 miles a day. The march from Edinburgh to Falkirk was long, however, fully 24 miles, and it seems likely that on this day Clifford and Beaumont's force, together with the heavy cavalry and other mounted elements of the vanguard, pressed on ahead of the main body of slow moving infantry and the baggage train. An interesting comparison can be made between the distances covered by Edward II's army and the progress of Henry III's army in April 1264. During the campaign that culminated in the battle of Lewes, what was probably a large army, marched from Grantham to Aylesbury, a distance of 80 miles as the crow flies in five days, an average of 16 miles a day. Chroniclers at the time were impressed by the speed of his march and mentioned nights with little sleep. King Henry and his cavalry pressed ahead and were in Croydon, fully 45 miles further on, when the infantry and baggage train reached Aylesbury. It seems probable that, as the English army approached the Scottish position in the New Park on 23 June, most of the horsemen, not only those of the vanguard, were to the fore and that the supporting infantry trailed well to the rear and the baggage train straggled miles behind.

The flat landscape of the Merse of Berwickshire with Hume Castle in the distance. Edward II's troops would have passed this way on 17 June 1314.

Meanwhile the Scots in the Torwood were drawn up in three divisions as for a withdrawal. Thomas Randolph, Earl of Moray, led the vanguard, the division nearest Stirling. The main-battle or centre, commanded by Edward Bruce, was positioned to the south of Moray. Furthest from Stirling and to the south of his brother's command was stationed King Robert with the rearguard. The Scottish cavalry brought warning that the English were approaching Falkirk and Bruce ordered a withdrawal from the Torwood. By evening the Scots had taken up positions in the New Park below Stirling Castle.

ORDERS OF BATTLE

THE BATTLE OF BANNOCKBURN, 23–24 JUNE 1314

THE ENGLISH ARMY
Commander-in-Chief – King Edward II

The Fore-Battle or Vanguard
Commanded jointly by Gilbert de Clare, Earl of Gloucester, and Humphrey de Bohun, Constable of England and Earl of Hereford.

Cavalry
600 Armoured Cavalry
250 Welsh mounted Troops (ie Hobelars) commanded by Sir Henry de Bohun.

Infantry
1,500 Longbowmen
150 Crossbowmen
1,500 Spearmen

The Main-Battle or Centre
Commanded by King Edward II

Cavalry
200 knights and men-at-arms riding ahead of the army as an advance guard under the Earl of Pembroke.
300 Cavalry commanded by Sir Robert Clifford
300 Cavalry of the King's Household, commanded by the seneschal, Sir Edmund Mauley

Infantry
2,500 Longbowmen
150 Crossbowmen
2,500 Spearmen

The Rear-Battle or Rearguard
Cavalry
600 Cavalry

Infantry
1,500 Longbowmen
150 Crossbowmen
1,500 Spearmen/Pikemen

Total: 2,000 Heavy Cavalry, 250 Light Cavalry 11,450 Infantry (Longbowmen, Crossbowmen, Spearmen)

THE SCOTTISH ARMY (23/6/1314)
Commander-in-Chief – King Robert I

The Rear-Battle or Rearguard (the Centre Division on 24 June)
Commanded by King Robert I.
4 sub-divisions totalling 2,400 pikemen

The Main-Battle or Centre (the Right Wing on 24 June)
Commanded by Edward Bruce, Earl of Carrick.
3 sub-divisions totalling 1,800 pikemen

The Fore-Battle or Vanguard (the left wing on 24 June)
Commanded by Thomas Randolph, Earl of Moray.
3 sub-divisions of pikemen totalling 1,800 pikemen

Light Cavalry
Commanded by James Douglas and Sir Robert Keith, Marshal of Scotland
350 Hobelars who fought as infantry

Archers
1,500 Archers.

Total: 7,500 Infantry, 350 light cavalry.

Note: I have calculated the numbers of the Scottish army from the minimum number of men that would be needed to cover half a mile of front, allowing each a frontage of 30 inches and standing in ranks six deep. There may have been many more Scots, perhaps as many as 10,000 men. I have divided the infantry into battalions or sub-divisions of 'schiltrons' of 600 men, although there is no concrete evidence for this organisation.

THE BATTLE OF BANNOCKBURN

The Terrain at Bannockburn

The Carse of Stirling, of which the Carse of Balquhiderock formed a part, was in 1314 a large area of flat, low-lying, boggy ground with areas of sodden peat. It was bordered to the north by the River Forth and to the south by a steep bank or escarpment, marked by the 20m contour at its base, which follows an almost straight line south-east from Stirling. Above this bank to the south-west the terrain is dryer and firmer, the ground undulating and wooded and rising gradually across two or three miles towards the higher and rougher moorland and hills around the headwaters of the Carron and Bannock Burn 500m above the carse. In addition to the springs that rise above the escarpment, all the surface water from the hills drained down into the flat peaty carse, which as a result was intersected in the 14th century by a large number of sluggish streams with deep peaty pools and overhanging crumbling banks, known by the Celtic word 'pols'. The entire Carse of Stirling was known at the time of the battle as 'les Polles' and would have presented a serious obstacle to a large army with its baggage train. The Carse of Stirling is mainly well-drained farmland today, the pols have largely disappeared, though the place names of the area betray their former existence.

The choice of route for the English army, approaching Stirling from the south-east, was thus extremely restricted. The only practical way was along the corridor of firm undulating country between the high moorland to the west and the boggy carse to the east. The ideal route was thus along the high road that ran through the middle of this area. Straddling the road was the wooded New Park, which was really a northerly continuation of the Torwood but was separated from it by the open, partly cultivated land of the Bannock Burn valley. The park had been fenced in by Alexander III in 1264 and was called New Park to distinguish it from the earlier King's Park below Stirling Castle. East of the New Park were the lands of the estate of Balquhiderock, which consisted partly of the cultivated Dryfield and partly of carseland. The Dryfield extends for about half a mile between the woodland of the park and the bank that falls steeply away to the boggy Carse of Balquhiderock, which lies between the Bannock Burn and the Pelstream Burn. Both these burns cross the Dryfield between high, steep banks, entangled with undergrowth and trees. The gorge of the Bannock Burn retains some of these features and remains impressive to this day. In 1314 the inhabited location above the gorge of the Bannock Burn was known as Bannock and

Medieval scribes, like this one at his lectern, are the source of much of our information. The imagination of the carver of this misericord in Worcester Cathedral has strayed into the realms of the fantastic, judging by the goings-on of his menagerie, a trait exhibited by some of the chroniclers themselves. (author's drawing)

later Bannockburn. There are divided opinions as to whether the battle took its name from this settlement or from the burn of the same name.

Contemporary Sources

There are three important English accounts of the battle; that in the *Vita Edwardi Secundi* by the well-informed Monk of Malmesbury may have been written as early as 1315. The *Chronicle of Lanercost*, an Augustinian Priory near Carlisle, includes an account that was probably written down at the time from information given by a Cumbrian knight who fought in the battle. In the *Scalacronica* of Sir Thomas Grey we have an account of Bannockburn from the author's father who fought in the battle. Though the chronicle was not compiled until 1355, the story of the battle must have been told to the author many times when he was a lad before he eventually set it down in writing. Of lesser importance are the *Annales Edwardi Secundi* of John de Trokelowe, written in about 1327, and Geoffrey le Baker's Chronicle of 1341. Both books describe the battle but are further removed from events, lack conviction and add little to the earlier accounts. The Canon of Bridlington, writing in the 1330s, has little of additional interest to add either.

From the Scots viewpoint the main source for Bannockburn is John Barbour, Archdeacon of Aberdeen, who completed his epic biographic poem *The Bruce* in 1376. It contains a lengthy and convincing description of the battle, which agrees in many respects with the accounts we have from the English sources. Barbour may have written 60 years after the battle, but for his account he drew on written sources that are now lost and on tales he had heard over the years from surviving veterans, though the only one he names is Sir Alan Cathcart, who told him of his adventures with Edward Bruce in Galloway. These are in fact the methods of any historian, ancient or modern. Barbour fills out the

Edward I stayed at Lanercost Priory during the winter of 1306/07 and it was here that the dying King condemned Thomas and Alexander Bruce to death as one of his last and most vindictive acts. The *Chronicle of Lanercost* preserves an eyewitness account of the battle of Bannockburn, probably from a Cumbrian knight who fought there.

The *Scalacronica* of Sir Thomas Grey of Heton on the Till, was written while he was languishing without a ransom as a prisoner in Edinburgh Castle. Only a broken remnant of Sir Thomas's castle now remains to remind us of the turbulent centuries of warfare on the Border. (photo Peter Ryder)

bare bones of the story with detail that brings the events to life but he has been accused of dramatic invention because his details are not corroborated by the other sparse accounts written nearer in time to the battle. The accounts in the *Vita*, *Lanercost* and the *Scalacronica* are all incomplete and exasperatingly sparing of detail. Even the most valuable source, the *Vita* is unbalanced by Malmesbury's fascination with the doings of Gloucester and his untimely demise. Whatever weight we choose to attach to John Barbour's account inevitably colours our view of the battle of Bannockburn.

Scots deployment – Saturday 22 June

The New Park was an enclosed, wooded hunting preserve about a mile from north to south by two miles from east to west. The park was set back half a mile north of the Bannock Burn at the point where the main road, along which the English were expected to advance, entered the woods. It was here, at the 'entry' to the New Park, that King Robert halted and drew up his rearguard in the open woodland. The Earl of Moray with the vanguard was to the north of the King's division at St Ninian's Kirk and Edward Bruce's division was positioned astride the road somewhere between the two. The Scots still retained their marching order for withdrawal, yet, hidden by the woods from the English, they were ideally positioned to oppose their advance, whether this came from the front or from the flank; in the event it came from both directions. The 'small folk', carters and camp followers, were sent away to a valley some way off, possibly one of the hollows below Coxet Hill, where they were safely out of the way as Bruce needed only his fighting men beside him as the English drew near.

Bruce ordered that a series of concealed pits or 'pottis' be dug, a foot in diameter and knee deep with a wooden stake in the bottom, to honeycomb the 'open field beside the road, where he thought the English would have to go if they wanted to move through the Park to the castle'. Evidently they were on either side of the road, where a frontal attack on the entry to the New Park might be expected. Curiously, apart from the fact that they were dug, there is no mention in any reliable source of their having any effect on the course of the fighting. Aerial photographs, taken during a particularly dry summer show what may be these pits across the Roman Road south of the entry. Recently, several sharpened wooden stakes that were found at Milton Bog in 1923 were re-examined and it is thought that they may be stakes from the bottom of the pits. It is hoped to carbon date them soon to confirm their age.

SUNDAY 23 JUNE 1314 – FIRST MOVES

Early on Sunday morning the Scots, still in the positions they had taken up the previous day, heard mass and in good heart awaited events. Douglas's and Keith's cavalry reconnoitred the advance of the English army from Falkirk. Sir Philip Moubray, the castellan of Stirling Castle, presumably with a safe-conduct from Robert Bruce, rode out to meet the King as he advanced by way of the Torwood. Moubray told Edward that now that the English army was within three leagues (6 miles) of Stirling Castle and had arrived before St John's Day, i.e. 24 June, the terms of his agreement with the Scots meant that the castle was now relieved, honour was satisfied and he need advance no further. It was probable that the Scots would retire without a fight and it might be well to await events advised Moubray, who was a Scot himself. He knew that Bruce was dangerous and warned Edward of the strength of the Scottish position in the New Park, where the woods had been made impassable by blocking the narrow pathways. Whether or not this cautious advice fell on deaf ears matters little as the forward troops, advancing impatiently drawn on by the withdrawing Scottish scouts, had taken on an independent momentum and were now beyond Edward's ineffectual control.

Meanwhile, Robert Bruce was concerned when he heard Douglas's report of the strength of the oncoming English and told him not to cause alarm, but rather to tell the troops that the English came on in

Panorama of the Bannock Burn valley looking north towards Stirling Castle from the English line of advance. The course of the Bannock Burn is marked by a line of trees in the middle distance.
1. Gillies Hill.
2. Ben Lomond.
3. Coxet Hill.
4. Flagpole and rotunda on site of the borestone.
5. Stirling Castle.
6. Ochil Hills.
(from NS799893)

The Bannock Burn valley from the Scottish position in front of the entry to the New Park. The course of the Bannock Burn is marked by a line of trees in the dip in the middle distance. (from NS796904)

great disorder. In fact this was true, the leading troops were pressing forward eagerly, leaving much of the army straggling and strung-out over many miles to the rear. The leadership similarly was in disarray as King Edward, in a foolish gesture of favouritism towards his nephew, the young Earl of Gloucester, had appointed him not only constable of the army on this occasion but also joint commander of the vanguard with Humphrey de Bohun, Earl of Hereford. The older and more experienced Hereford was by right the hereditary Constable of England. As neighbouring lords of the Welsh Marches, there was a long-standing and bitter rivalry between the De Bohuns of Brecknock and the Clares of Glamorgan. By advancing Gloucester's pretensions to command, with a contempt for military considerations, Edward undermined Hereford and left the English van without decisive direction.

Bruce versus Henry de Bohun

The afternoon shadows were lengthening when Edward and his entourage halted to decide whether the army should take up quarters for the night or fight that day. The vanguard knew nothing of this delay but rode on towards the New Park. As they emerged from the Torwood they saw the Scottish mounted reconnaissance force withdrawing before them and spurred their mounts forward in pursuit towards the entry to the New Park. To the fore was the Earl of Hereford with his strong retinue of knights and men-at-arms, among whom were his brother Gilbert and his hot-blooded nephew Henry. As the leading groups of horsemen crossed the open valley of the Bannock Burn, the Scots pikemen began to emerge from the woods ahead and form up to oppose their advance. Henry de Bohun was a good bow-shot to the fore and, as he drew rein before the Scots, he sighted a knight mounted on a spirited grey palfrey, arraying his pikemen with an axe in his hand; the double tressured lion of his surcoat and the glint of gold from the crown encircling his bascinet identified him as the Bruce. De Bohun, sensing that his moment of glory had come, wheeled his charger and spurred towards the king with an arrogant taunt on his lips. Bruce set his horse towards his challenger, who bore down full-tilt. As they closed Bruce swerved his nimble horse aside to avoid de Bohun's lance and, standing in his stirrups, struck him such a blow with his axe that it cleaved through the English knight's helmet and bit deep into his brain. The axe shaft shattered with the impact and De Bohun crashed from the saddle, dead before he hit the ground. His gallant squire was killed standing over his fallen master as the eager Scots pressed forward, emboldened by King Robert's portentous feat of arms. The ranks of pikemen formed an impenetrable, bristling hedge of steel-tipped pikes against which the charge of the horsemen of the English vanguard, far outstripping their infantry support, foundered in bloody confusion. Gloucester, at the head of his troops, was dragged to safety as his horse was killed under him in the thick of the fray. Then, as Edward Bruce's division debouched from the woods in support of the battling rearguard, the English fell back. With a great shout, the Scots surged forwards and the English horsemen turned and fled, beaten and in disorder. The Scots pursued them but the well-mounted English escaped with little further loss. Bruce recalled his men and withdrew to the safety of the wooded New Park. Those Scots lords with the King who dared speak out, remonstrated with him for the risk he had taken in accepting de Bohun's challenge, which could have been fatal to their cause. The Bruce made no answer but bemoaned the loss of his good battle-axe.

The *Vita* gives a rather less heroic account of the duel. ' ... Henry, seeing he could not resist the multitude of the Scots, turned his horse with the intention of returning to his companions; but Robert opposed him and struck him on the head with an axe ... his squire trying to protect or rescue his lord was overwhelmed by the Scots.'

Clifford Repulsed

As Gloucester and Hereford's horsemen pressed on along the main road towards the entry to the New Park, a strong mounted force under Sir Robert Clifford spurred to the fore and rode north towards Stirling, aiming to skirt round the New Park and win through to the castle, past the Scottish left flank. Estimates of the strength of this mounted squadron vary, but it was far more than a patrol or raiding party, it was undoubtedly a formidable fighting force. Barbour says there were 800 horse under four bannerets, including Clifford, Sir Henry Beaumont and the Yorkshire knight Sir Miles Stapleton. Sir Thomas Grey, whose father, Sir Thomas Grey the elder of Heaton on the Till, rode with Clifford's cavalry force, tells of only 300 horsemen and, as he was there, we must incline to his figure. It may be that Clifford's force was intended to carry out a reconnaissance in strength to see if the army could reach Stirling without passing through the New Park. However,

OVERLEAF **Henry de Bohun, hot-blooded nephew of the Earl of Hereford, was at the forefront of the English vanguard as it emerged from the Torwood. Catching sight of Robert Bruce arraying his pikemen, De Bohun spurred his charger towards the Scottish King. Scorning flight Bruce turned his grey palfrey towards his challenger and as De Bohun thundered towards him nimbly swerved aside. Standing in his stirrups he brought his battle-axe crashing down on the helmet of his opponent. The blow cut through the helm and bit deep into the brain of the impetuous young knight, killing him instantly and shattering the shaft of the axe. De Bohun's squire was killed defending his fallen master's body. The Scots lords chastised their king for taking such a risk, but Bruce remained unrepentant, lamenting only the loss of a good axe. (Graham Turner)**

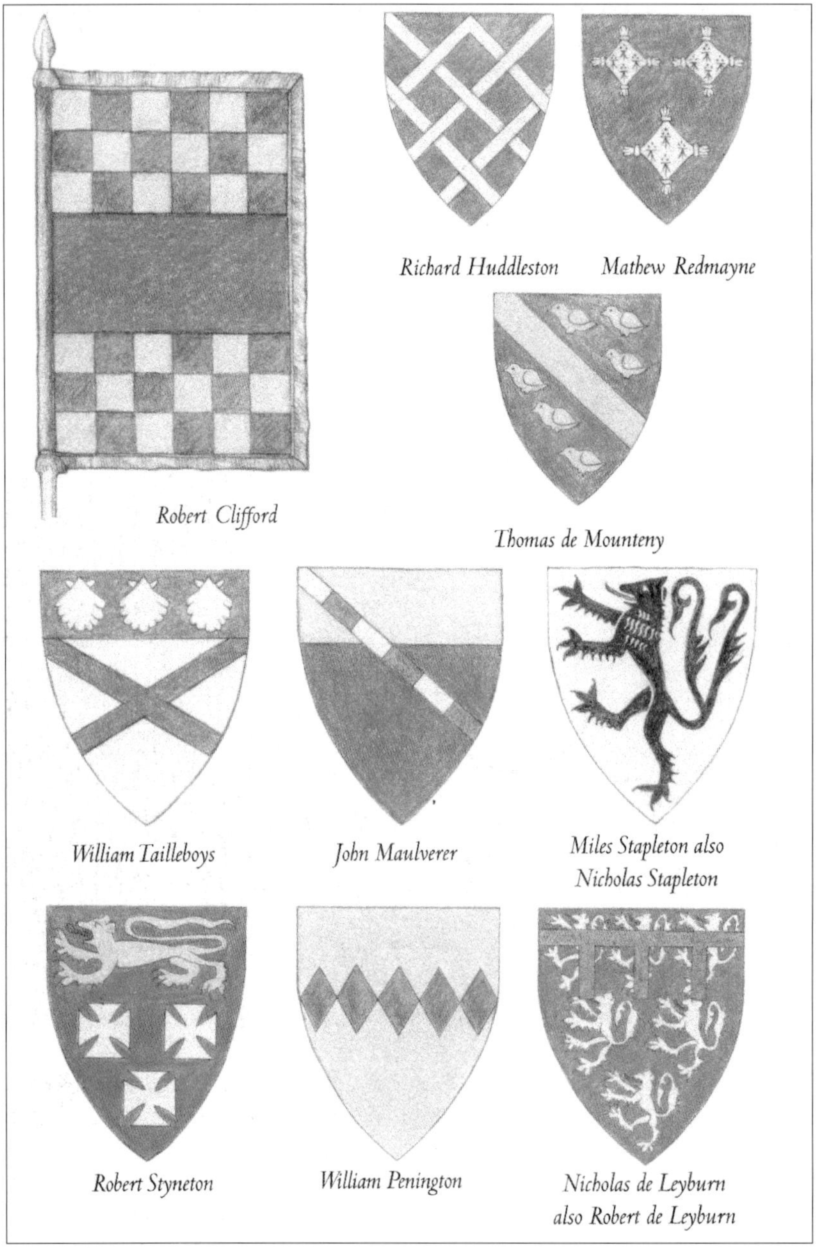

Robert Clifford
Richard Huddleston
Mathew Redmayne
Thomas de Mounteny
William Tailleboys
John Maulverer
Miles Stapleton also
Nicholas Stapleton
Robert Styneton
William Penington
Nicholas de Leyburn
also Robert de Leyburn

Arms of the knights of Sir Robert Clifford's retinue at the battle of Bannockburn. (illustration by Lyn Armstrong)

this is not confirmed by contemporary writers. Grey offers no explanation. Barbour says that Clifford's task was to 'go to the castle, for if they could indeed reach there, they thought it would be rescued'. According to the Lanercost Chronicle, Clifford, 'wished to ride round the wood to prevent the Scots escaping by flight'. It seems that the English at this stage were still confident that the Scots did not intend to fight a pitched battle outside Stirling. We cannot be sure what Clifford's intentions were, it is possible that his advance was as independent of the King's direction as that of Gloucester and Hereford. However, we can be sure that there was neither liaison nor co-ordination between these advance units of the English army, and both may have started out under the delusion that they were pursuing an enemy in full retreat.

Clifford's force, as both Grey and Barbour emphasise, rode in the open fields, well clear of the trees of the New Park, towards Stirling. The route they took was most probably along the track known as 'the Way', which skirted the escarpment along the flat carse and led to a ford where the Bannock Burn issued from its gorge on to the Carse of Balquhiderock. They rode past St Ninian's Kirk, below which the boggy Pelstream Burn flows into the carse. They were unopposed and must have thought their way to Stirling was clear. However, the Earl of Moray's division was posted near St Ninian's to guard the main road north against a flanking movement such as this by the English. Bruce made no dispositions to cover an advance further out on the carse, so presumably he considered the terrain there impractical. Clifford had passed below Moray's position before the earl responded, earning King Robert's displeasure who told the earl bluntly that 'a rose had fallen from his chaplet'. Moray was annoyed and angry with himself and set about restoring the situation, and with no more than 500 hastily assembled men he hurried to confront Clifford. At the sight of the Scots pouring from the New Park into the open, the English drew rein and at Beaumont's insistence, confidently allowed them room to come on, away from the shelter of the woods. Moray saw the danger of envelopment

2. PHASE 1. Robert Bruce's schiltron, probably about 2,500 men, mostly pikemen supported by archers, defend the 'entry'. It is here that the famous duel between Robert Bruce and Henry de Bohun takes place.

3. PHASE 1. Edward Bruce, with about 1,800 men deployed near the borestone, moves his schiltron to support his brother and to guard the western approaches to the New Park as English cavalry are probing this area.

4. PHASE 1. Douglas's and Keith's reconnaissance forces dismount. Their light cavalry role is over and they will now fight as infantry. Douglas moves north to support Moray while Keith fights alongside Edward Bruce.

9. PHASE 1. The mounted troops of the English Vanguard under the joint command of the earls of Hereford and Gloucester outstrip the main force and are confronted by Robert Bruce's schiltron at the 'entry' to the New Park. There is fierce fighting in which Gloucester's horse is killed and the English are repulsed.

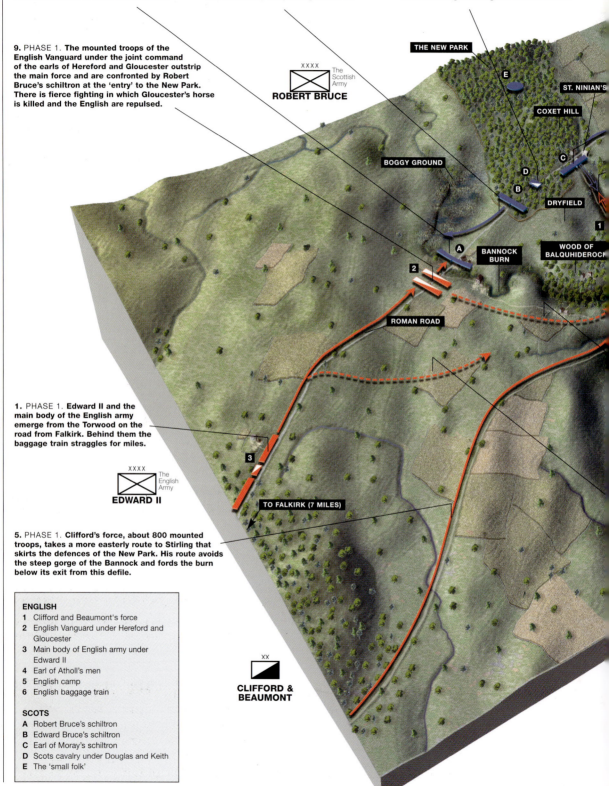

THE NEW PARK

ST. NINIAN'S

COXET HILL

E

D

BOGGY GROUND

B

C

DRYFIELD

ROBERT BRUCE
XXXX
The Scottish Army

A

BANNOCK BURN

WOOD OF BALQUHIDEROCK

1

2

ROMAN ROAD

1. PHASE 1. Edward II and the main body of the English army emerge from the Torwood on the road from Falkirk. Behind them the baggage train straggles for miles.

3

EDWARD II
XXXX
The English Army

TO FALKIRK (7 MILES)

5. PHASE 1. Clifford's force, about 800 mounted troops, takes a more easterly route to Stirling that skirts the defences of the New Park. His route avoids the steep gorge of the Bannock and fords the burn below its exit from this defile.

CLIFFORD & BEAUMONT
XX

ENGLISH
1 Clifford and Beaumont's force
2 English Vanguard under Hereford and Gloucester
3 Main body of English army under Edward II
4 Earl of Atholl's men
5 English camp
6 English baggage train

SCOTS
A Robert Bruce's schiltron
B Edward Bruce's schiltron
C Earl of Moray's schiltron
D Scots cavalry under Douglas and Keith
E The 'small folk'

54

7. PHASE 1. Moray may well not have seen Clifford's advance along 'The Way' until very late. The Wood of Balquhiderock would have blocked his view. He did not react until Clifford was almost abreast of his position. He then ordered his pikemen to intercept the English. It was this apparent tardiness that earned Moray his rebuke from Robert Bruce, 'For the King haid said rudly That a rose of his chaplete was fallyn'.

8. PHASE 1. Clifford's force is confronted by the Earl of Moray's schiltron of at least 1,800 men, which issues from the woods by St Ninian's. The English are defeated, some escape north towards Stirling Castle, others ride back to the main body of the army.

8a. The alternative site for the clash between Clifford and Moray is on the Dryfield of Balquhiderock.

14. PHASE 3. Night of 23/24 June. The renegade Earl of Atholl attacks the Scottish supply depot at Cambuskenneth.

6. PHASE 1. Clifford may have followed 'The Way' across the Dryfield of Balquhiderock towards its junction with the Stirling road or, as seems more likely, continued north along the Carse.

13. PHASE 2. Edward II and the English cavalry camp on the Carse of Balquhiderock. The army is dispersed and uncomfortable.

12. PHASE 2. The baggage train of at least 200 wagons straggles into camp throughout the evening. The baggage train and the majority of the infantry do not cross the Bannock Burn, but make camp in the Carse of Skeoch.

10. PHASE 2. Gloucester and Hereford's cavalry, defeated at the 'entry', make for the Carse of Balquhiderock to camp for the night. This allows them to water their horses.

11. PHASE 2. Edward II and the main body of the English army also make for the Carse as they are denied a way through the New Park to their preferred camping ground in the shadow of Stirling Castle.

THE FIGHTING ON 23 JUNE

Sunday 23 June 1314, early afternoon to evening, viewed from the southeast showing the first contact between the armies. The Scots are deployed as if for withdrawal. Gloucester and Hereford attempt to force a way through to Stirling at the 'entry' to the New Park. Clifford and Beaumont skirt the New Park along 'the Way', which runs along the Carse below the escarpment, where their progress is blocked by the Earl of Moray and his pikemen.

The numbered markers in the image are labelled 1, 2, 3, 4.

View from the Carse of Skioch across the Caledonian Railway towards the re-entrant of the Bannock Burn valley, showing the slope of the steep escarpment that rises from the carse.
1. Bannockburn.
2. The escarpment.
3. Re-entrant of the Bannock Burn.
4. The Dryfield of Balquhiderock.
(from NS820910)

by the English cavalry and turned his rear ranks about so that his formation bristled with spears to both front and rear. Sir Thomas Grey remonstrated with Beaumont on account of his overconfidence but was peremptorily rebuked with an accusation of cowardice. Stung by this taunt, Thomas spurred his mount recklessly between Beaumont and Sir William Deyncourt and charged into the thick of the enemy. Deyncourt followed rashly and both his horse and that of Sir Thomas Grey were pierced by the pikes. Thomas was dragged inside the schiltron and taken prisoner, but the unfortunate Deyncourt was killed along with his young brother Reginald. The rest of the horsemen came on together with more deliberation, surrounding the Scots, but were unable to break into their tight, disciplined formation. The Scots piked the horses that came near them and killed the riders as they fell, while others darted out from the ranks to stab horses and bring down the knights. Without the support of archers, Clifford's horsemen were unable to break up the Scottish schiltron and in frustration 'they threw swords and maces so fiercely among them that there was a mountain of weapons amidst them'. Barbour says that James Douglas at this point asked King Robert's permission to go to the assistance of the hard-pressed Earl of Moray, but his request was refused. Then, without explanation, Barbour tells us that Bruce changed his mind and that Douglas and his men, presumably still mounted at this stage, hurried to the aid of the outnumbered earl. Yet, if we are to believe Sir Thomas Grey, it was the English who were outnumbered! When the English saw this new threat near at hand they fell back and Douglas, seeing that Clifford's attack was faltering, chivalrously held his men back to allow Moray to complete his victory.

Robert Bruce, King of Scots, at
the battle of Bannockburn.
(model by the author)

Some survivors of Clifford's force rode headlong towards Stirling
Castle and others, including Clifford himself, fled back the way they had
come to the main body of the English army. The Monk of Malmesbury
tells us that Clifford was killed the following day along with Gloucester,
Payn Tibetot and William Marshall. Clifford was, after the Earl of
Gloucester, the most prominent of those killed at Bannockburn. He had
a retinue of 50 knights and men-at-arms of whom the names of 13 are
known to us, of these only Sir Miles Stapleton seems to have been killed
in the battle.

Results of the first day's fighting
The defeat of Clifford's cavalry brought the fighting of 23 June to an
end; it was late in the day and no further attempt was made to break
through to Stirling Castle. This setback, following close upon the
repulse of the Earls of Hereford and Gloucester, spread gloom and
discouragement throughout the ranks of the English army. The
importance of the large-scale action that resulted in the defeat of the
English vanguard has been overshadowed in contemporary accounts by
the celebrated tale of the confrontation between Robert Bruce and
Henry de Bohun. The duel has an exact counterpart in the single

combat described by Geofrey le Baker before the battle of Halidon Hill, where again the outcome foreshadows the result of the battle.

Sir Thomas Grey, our eyewitness, though he was in the hands of the Scots by the evening of the 23rd, says that the events of the day had damaged the confidence and resolve of the English. It is possible, however, that the discouragement of the English has been overstated in the light of the following day's defeat. Only a fraction of the English host had been in contact with the enemy and most had not even seen the Scots. Many, according to John of Trokelowe, were bitter against the Scots because of their repulse and vowed to be revenged on the morrow.

Moray's victory not only stopped the English opening a route to Stirling Castle but also, and more importantly, it demonstrated the effectiveness of the Scots pikemen against the English horsemen. It is highly likely that Edward II's plan was for his army to camp in the shadow of Stirling Castle in the King's Park on the night of the 23/24 June. He had expected the Scots to either retreat before him without a fight or to be easily brushed aside. Now, with the day drawing to a close, his plans were thwarted and awry. Two of his formations had been mauled and repulsed by the Scots and his route to Stirling and his planned camping-ground was blocked. The English army needed a place to set down for the night, as the men were hungry and exhausted by the long march and the horses needed to be watered. It was decided to put all the cavalry and possibly some part of the infantry across the Bannock Burn on to the Carse of Balquhiderock where the horses would find a plentiful supply of water and the men could rest for the night.

The carse was not where the English had planned to spend the night; Grey calls it an evil, deep marsh with streams and there is no doubt that at the time of the battle it was a wetter and boggier place than today. Barbour says that because there were 'pows' or sluggish streams in the carse they broke down houses and roofing and carried off wood to make bridges by which to cross the streams. He places this activity after dark, which is not until midnight at this time of year in the north. The English spent a wakeful and anxious night; the horses bridled and the men armed, alerted by the aggressiveness of the Scots to the possibility of a night attack. Edward II must have appreciated the awkwardness of his position and realised that there was a possibility of continued fighting on the following day, but there was nothing at this late hour he could do to improve the situation. It is likely that the main body of the English infantry did not cross the Bannock Burn on to the congested carse but spent the night in the area south of the burn, bivouacking in some disorder as they arrived late in the evening from the direction of Falkirk.

Meanwhile, as the English floundered on the carse, Robert Bruce called his officers together for a council of war. He was much encouraged by the successes of the day, his plans were intact and his army flushed with victory. Yet his deep-rooted caution urged him to withdraw to the rugged fastness of the Lennox, where the country was too wild for the English to follow. Harsh experience had taught Bruce to avoid pitched battles and inclined him towards the less knightly yet effective policy of irregular warfare. The divisions of the Scots army were still positioned as for a withdrawal when, during the hours of darkness, a Scots knight in English service, Sir Alexander Seton, took advantage of the confusion in the English camp to slip away and make his way to Robert Bruce's

headquarters. Seton told Bruce of the disorganised condition of the English and of their discouragement and lack of leadership and pledged his life that if Bruce attacked in the morning he would have victory. Barbour tells us that King Robert turned to his officers to ask if they should fight or not and that with one voice they boldly answered for battle. It must have been at this moment that King Robert decided to risk all on a battle in the morning. Abbot Bernard of Arbroath was present, he had brought the famous Reliquary of Saint Columba with him to inspire the Scots army. He recorded the inspiring words with which Robert Bruce addressed his officers on the eve of Bannockburn and clearly they made a profound impression on all present.

THE SITE OF THE BATTLE

The events of the first day's fighting can be described with some confidence and without too many inconsistencies. It is in describing the events of the second day's fighting, the climax of the battle, that difficulties occur. My description of the battle, which follows, places it on the Dryfield of Balquhiderock, but opinion is divided on this and many favour the Carse of Balquhiderock as the site. Deciding between these two possible sites is difficult because of the changes to the landscape that have been wrought over the centuries. There was undoubtedly more woodland in 1314. Bogs and marshes were then far more extensive and the Carse of Balquhiderock was certainly not the well-drained almost manicured farmland that we see today.

We know from Sir Thomas Grey that, 'The English columns … were jammed together and could not operate against them [the Scots].' Lanercost says something similar: 'The English in the rear could not reach the Scots because the leading division was in the way.' This state of affairs must have been because the nature of the ground restricted and hemmed in the English, so they were unable to deploy their superior numbers or bring their archers into action. The topography of both the Dryfield and the Carse of Balquhiderock can be made to fit the situation.

On the carse, the Bannock Burn and the Pelstream Burn have to be the restricting features, at their nearest approach they are about half a mile apart. The Pelstream Burn, however, may not run its original course on the carse and any associated bogs and marshland that once existed have been drained, so there is no more than a rather unconvincing stream to be seen today.

On the alternative Dryfield site, the Pelstream burn crosses the Dryfield in a deep, steep-sided channel that even today in parts retains enough of its former cover of trees and entangled undergrowth to suggest that it would have prevented the passage of formed bodies of troops in 1314. This forms the northern extremity of the Dryfield battle site. To the south the Wood of Balquhiderock, though reduced from its former extent, still covers the steep escarpment and forms an obstacle to progress between the carse and the Dryfield between the point where the Bannock Burn disgorges on to the carse and the settlement of Broomridge. Between Broomridge and the Pelstream Burn the contours widen enough to allow easy access to the Dryfield, and it is this gap through which the English heavy cavalry made their way on 24 June to

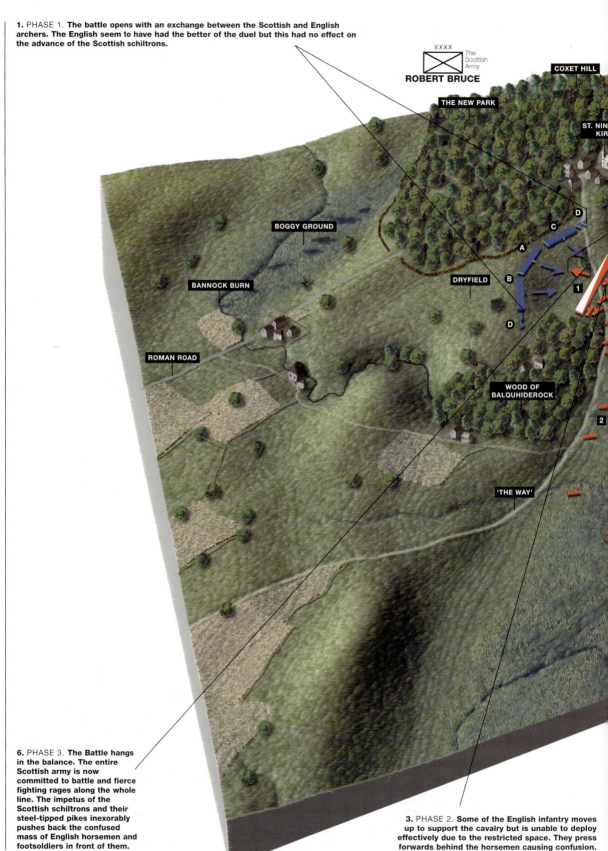

1. PHASE 1. **The battle opens with an exchange between the Scottish and English archers. The English seem to have had the better of the duel but this had no effect on the advance of the Scottish schiltrons.**

xxxx
The Scottish Army
ROBERT BRUCE

COXET HILL

THE NEW PARK

ST. NIN KIR

BOGGY GROUND

BANNOCK BURN

DRYFIELD

A

B

C

D

D

1

ROMAN ROAD

WOOD OF BALQUHIDEROCK

2

'THE WAY'

6. PHASE 3. **The Battle hangs in the balance. The entire Scottish army is now committed to battle and fierce fighting rages along the whole line. The impetus of the Scottish schiltrons and their steel-tipped pikes inexorably pushes back the confused mass of English horsemen and footsoldiers in front of them.**

62

3. PHASE 2. **Some of the English infantry moves up to support the cavalry but is unable to deploy effectively due to the restricted space. They press forwards behind the horsemen causing confusion.**

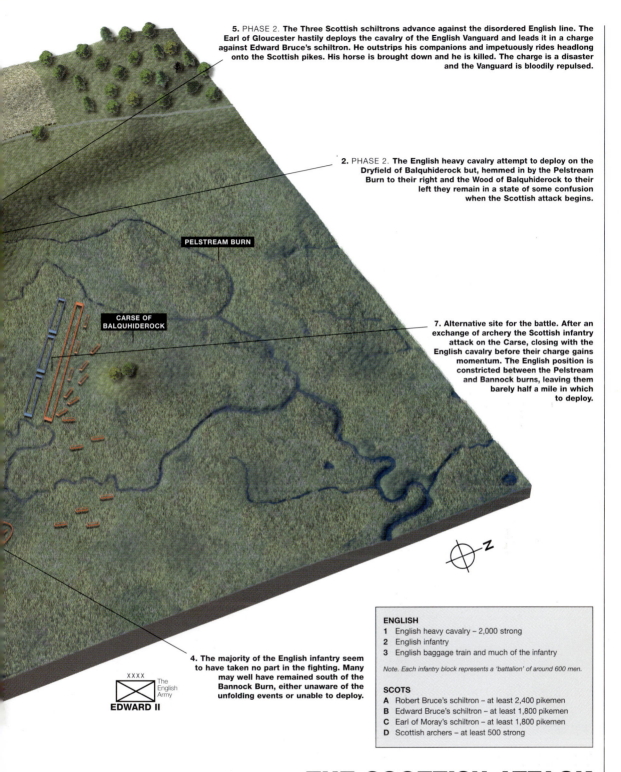

5. PHASE 2. The Three Scottish schiltrons advance against the disordered English line. The Earl of Gloucester hastily deploys the cavalry of the English Vanguard and leads it in a charge against Edward Bruce's schiltron. He outstrips his companions and impetuously rides headlong onto the Scottish pikes. His horse is brought down and he is killed. The charge is a disaster and the Vanguard is bloodily repulsed.

2. PHASE 2. The English heavy cavalry attempt to deploy on the Dryfield of Balquhiderock but, hemmed in by the Pelstream Burn to their right and the Wood of Balquhiderock to their left they remain in a state of some confusion when the Scottish attack begins.

PELSTREAM BURN

CARSE OF
BALQUHIDEROCK

7. Alternative site for the battle. After an exchange of archery the Scottish infantry attack on the Carse, closing with the English cavalry before their charge gains momentum. The English position is constricted between the Pelstream and Bannock burns, leaving them barely half a mile in which to deploy.

4. The majority of the English infantry seem to have taken no part in the fighting. Many may well have remained south of the Bannock Burn, either unaware of the unfolding events or unable to deploy.

XXXX
The
English
Army
EDWARD II

ENGLISH
1   English heavy cavalry – 2,000 strong
2   English infantry
3   English baggage train and much of the infantry

Note. Each infantry block represents a 'battalion' of around 600 men.

SCOTS
A   Robert Bruce's schiltron – at least 2,400 pikemen
B   Edward Bruce's schiltron – at least 1,800 pikemen
C   Earl of Moray's schiltron – at least 1,800 pikemen
D   Scottish archers – at least 500 strong

THE SCOTTISH ATTACK

Monday 24 June 1314, early morning, viewed from the southeast. After a brief and inconclusive archery duel, the Scots attack the English cavalry who are forming up on the Dryfield. The Earl of Gloucester leads the cavalry of the English vanguard in an impetuous, and disastrous, charge against Edward Bruce's schiltron. The Scottish pikemen close on the disorganised English line and a bloody mêlée develops.

form up on a line north-west to south-east, facing the New Park. The former extent of the Wood of Balquhiderock on the Dryfield is not clear but we must assume that it was more extensive than today and served to restrict the width of the battlefield to the south.

If this was the case then the English may have been pushed back from the Dryfield into a narrowing funnel formed by the Wood of Balquhiderock and the Pelstream Burn, which resulted in their being increasingly bunched together into a constricted mass. From this followed defeat and flight via the carse to their rear along which they could escape either north, towards Stirling Castle, or in the direction of the River Forth or back over the Bannock Burn. This fits in nicely with what we know about the flight of the English from the battlefield. Yet the uncertainty surrounding the defining features of the landscape in the early fourteenth century leaves the site of the battle still tantalisingly elusive. Despite the continuing urbanisation of the Dryfield site, a visit is interesting and worthwhile. It is still possible to walk over the area, the features mentioned are still there, and with a little imagination readers can form their own opinions on the site of the battle.

DAWN, MONDAY 24 JUNE 1314 – THE SCOTS ATTACK

As first light began to illuminate the sky over the Firth of Forth at about 3.15a.m. on that fateful Monday, in the woods of the New Park the Scots prepared themselves for battle. King Robert gave orders for a dawn attack, and the disciplined formations of pikemen drew up in the open under the banners of their leaders. There, in full view of the enemy, the Scots knelt briefly to say the Lord's Prayer and for every man to commend his soul to God.

The English cavalry had taken advantage of the easier contours of the land between the Pelstream Burn and the Wood of Balquhiderock to begin to establish themselves on the firm ground or dryfield above the 20m contour. They were glad to leave the sodden Carse of Balquhiderock and though they were anticipating opposition to their advance they were not expecting the Scots to issue from their wooded stronghold and attack them. The division of Edward Bruce, which had probably been stationed somewhere between the Borestone and Saint Ninian's, was on the right of the Scottish line and had the honour of leading the attack. On his left and slightly in echelon behind, was the division of King Robert. The Earl of Moray's division made up the left wing of the Scottish host, but to the English they appeared as one huge mass of advancing men. King Edward watched as the Scots infantry emerged from the woods and apparently still unaware that they meant to attack asked, 'What, will yon Scots fight?' Sir Ingram d'Umfraville, a Scot himself, assured the King that they would. When the Scots paused and knelt to pray, Edward, according to Barbour, mistook the situation and told Umfraville, 'Yon folk kneel to ask mercy.'

'They ask mercy, surely, but not from you. They ask God for mercy for their sins,' replied Sir Ingram, 'Yon men will win all, or die; none will flee for fear of death.' Umfraville and several of the older more

experienced knights, who appreciated the fighting qualities of the Scots, had advised delaying the advance for a day because of the state of the army after its long march north. Gloucester, who shared their opinion, had put this to the King but the younger knights called this good advice cowardice and Edward rebuffed the Earl, hotly accusing him of treachery. Umfraville's tactical advice to the King, which involved a feigned withdrawal, was impractical and potentially disastrous and Edward, rightly for once, rejected it. It was too late for such niceties anyway, the initiative had passed to the Scots, the English had no choice, they were in a tight corner and must fight their way out of it.

The Lanercost Chronicle, which contains the report of an eyewitness, says that before the Scots infantry closed with the enemy, 'the English archers were thrown forward before the line and the Scottish archers engaged them, a few being killed and wounded on either side; but the King of England's archers quickly put the others to flight.' This exchange seems to have been an isolated affair of archers, and it had no effect on the advance of the Scots pikemen. The Scots archers may have been discomforted in this early exchange but they were by no means defeated and it may have been their fire that tipped the scales at the climax of the battle. Their contribution to the victory has been much undervalued.

As the Scots infantry surged towards the still disorganised English to their front, Gloucester hastily formed up the cavalry of the vanguard and with himself at their head, charged the leading schiltron of Edward Bruce. The impetuous Earl outstripped his support and rode headlong on to the pikes of the Scots, his horse was brought down and he was killed. It is said that he had armed in haste and had no heraldic surcoat over his armour so, unrecognised, he was despatched by the pikemen. Thus, as Robert Bruce later lamented, was a princely ransom lost. Gloucester's charge was a disastrous failure and the English vanguard was tumbled in bloody confusion before the impenetrable forest of pikes.

The two Scots divisions advancing on Edward Bruce's left came into contact almost simultaneously with the disordered English line to their front, which was little more than a great mass of men bunched together in confusion, 'all in a schiltrom' as Barbour puts it. Grey describes the English as, 'jammed together' and, as stated previously, Lanercost says much the same.

It seems from this that some of the English infantry had come up but were unable to deploy because of the restricted space between the entangled woodland covering the steep-sided channel of the Pelstream Burn and the Wood of Balquhiderock and were pressing forward behind the horsemen, causing confusion. The majority of the English

Panorama of the Carse of Stirling looking towards the castle from the south-east. The Bannock Burn flows immediately behind Redhall Farm on the left of the view.
1. Gillies Hill.
2. Redhall Farm.
3. Stirling Castle.
4. Ben Ledi.
5. Wallace Memorial on the Abbey Craig.
6. Viewpoint NS824919.
7. Ochil Hills.

OVERLEAF As the pikemen of the Scottish schiltrons surged to the attack on the morning of 24 June, Gilbert de Clare, Earl of Gloucester, hastily gathered the cavalry of the English vanguard and led them to the attack. With himself at their head Gloucester launched the cavalry at the leading schiltron commanded by Edward Bruce. The result was a disastrous and bloody failure; The English cavalry was unable to penetrate the hedge of pikes and recoiled in confusion. Gloucester himself was unhorsed and killed. Having armed quickly he did not wear his heraldic surcoat, which would probably have saved him as the value of his ransom would have meant his life was spared. (Graham Turner)

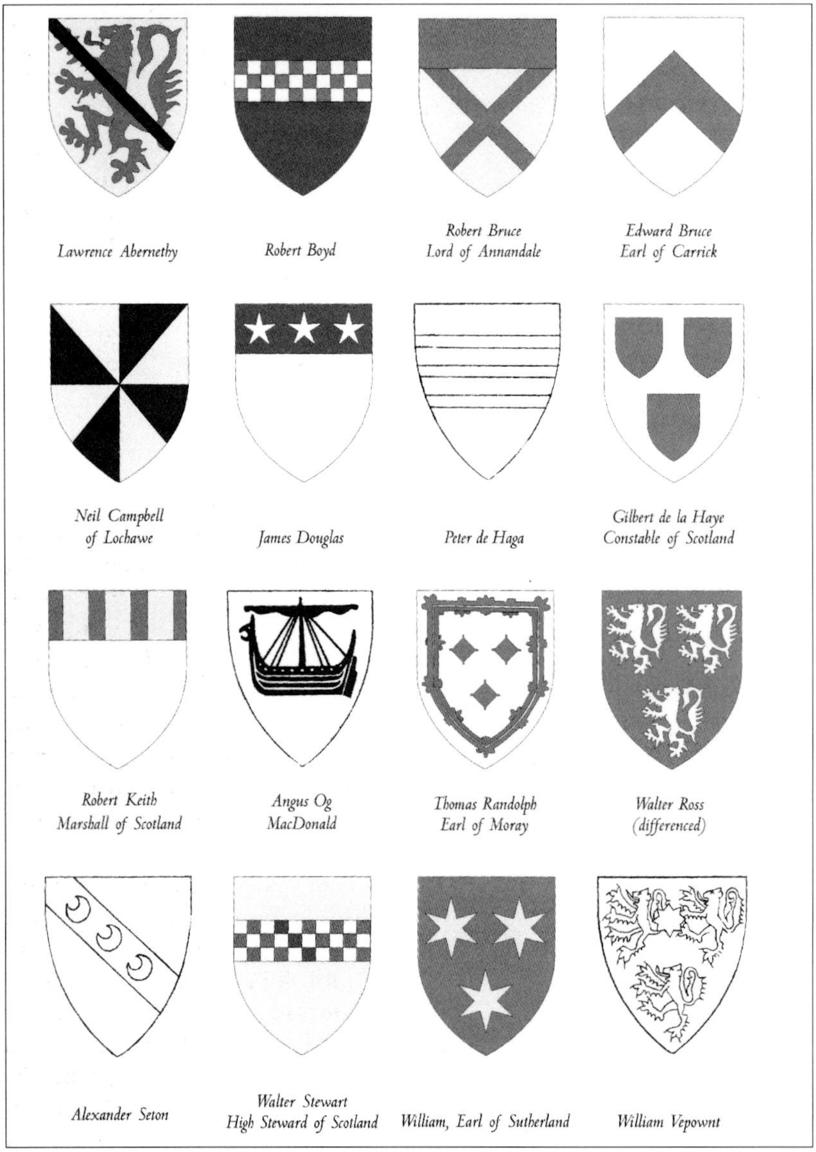

Lawrence Abernethy
Robert Boyd
Robert Bruce
Lord of Annandale
Edward Bruce
Earl of Carrick
Neil Campbell
of Lochawe
James Douglas
Peter de Haga
Gilbert de la Haye
Constable of Scotland
Robert Keith
Marshall of Scotland
Angus Og
MacDonald
Thomas Randolph
Earl of Moray
Walter Ross
(differenced)
Alexander Seton
Walter Stewart
High Steward of Scotland
William, Earl of Sutherland
William Vepownt

Arms of the Scottish knights who fought for Robert Bruce at Bannockburn. (illustration by Lyn Armstrong)

infantry, for this reason, seem to have taken no part in the fighting, though it may be that many remained south of the Bannock Burn enshrouded by the fog of war and knew nothing of the drama unfolding out of their line of sight. Meanwhile, a dangerous number of English archers had managed to take up position on the flank of the mêlée and commenced a galling fire, 'so fast that if their shooting had persisted it would have gone hard for the Scots', wrote Barbour. Robert Bruce knew, better than the English leaders themselves it seems, the danger posed by the bowmen and ordered the Marischal, Sir Robert Keith, who was held in reserve, to attack them with his light-horse. Their charge was delivered with such effect that the archers were scattered and driven headlong into the ranks of those advancing from the rear, causing more confusion and alarm.

For a moment the outcome of the battle hung in the balance, the entire strength of the Scottish army was now committed to battle and fighting raged fiercely along the whole front. The air filled with the din of battle as inexorably the weight of the steel-tipped schiltrons bore down on the confused mass of entangled horsemen and foot before them. The English were jammed together so closely that there was barely room to wield their weapons and those that fell were trampled underfoot in the press. The Scots archers, emboldened by the defeat of the English bowmen, poured a deadly hail of arrows into the struggling mass of the enemy. The English began to give ground, gradually at first, then their resistance crumbled and the trickle of men making their way to the rear became a torrent as they broke and fled. At this, a great shout of triumph went up from the ranks of the Scots and the schiltrons surged forwards.

MID-MORNING – THE ENGLISH DEFEATED

The battle was past saving for the English, and the defeated troops thought only of survival and escape. At this moment in the rear of the attacking Scots appeared a mob of non-combatants, wagoners, cooks, camp followers and servants; the 'small folk', who had been sent away by Robert Bruce before the battle to the safety of a hollow to the north of Coxet Hill. Now with makeshift weapons and improvised banners they streamed towards the rout with bloodthirsty cries. Their intervention had little or no effect on the outcome of the battle, though the fleeing English may have thought they were fresh reinforcements arriving and redoubled their efforts to escape. Robert Bruce can hardly have welcomed the arrival of this undisciplined, plundering rabble who would prove a hindrance if unrestrained.

When the English leaders saw that all was lost, the Earl of Pembroke and Sir Giles d'Argentan, who were at King Edward's side, realised that his safety was vital and that he must not fall into the hands of the Scots as the repercussions of his capture were unthinkable. Much against his will the King was led from the field, in the nick of time, towards the safety of Stirling Castle, for the way along the edge of the carse was still open. The Scots laid hold of the covering of the King's charger but he struck out and felled them with his mace. He had one horse killed under him before he fought his way free though his trusty shield-bearer, Sir Roger Northburgh, was brought down and captured. Once clear of the fighting, the King rode for the castle accompanied by Pembroke and a large body of horsemen. As soon as he saw the King out of danger Giles d'Argentan, fearful for his honour and unaccustomed to flight, turned his mount and plunged back into the thick of the fighting where he was killed. The flight of Edward II from the battlefield signalled the break-up of the English army. Some followed the King towards Stirling, others fled across the carse towards the River Forth but it was impassable and many drowned attempting to cross. The disorderly mass of men that fled south were thrown into confusion as they attempted to pass the Bannock Burn. The passage of thousands had churned the banks of the burn into a sea of treacherous mud and set a trap into which the fleeing mass of men, carried forward by the great press behind, tumbled headlong and perished. It was here that the beaten army suffered some of its heaviest losses, including the King's seneschal, Sir Edmund Mauley. Barbour paints a vivid word-picture of the Bannock Burn, so

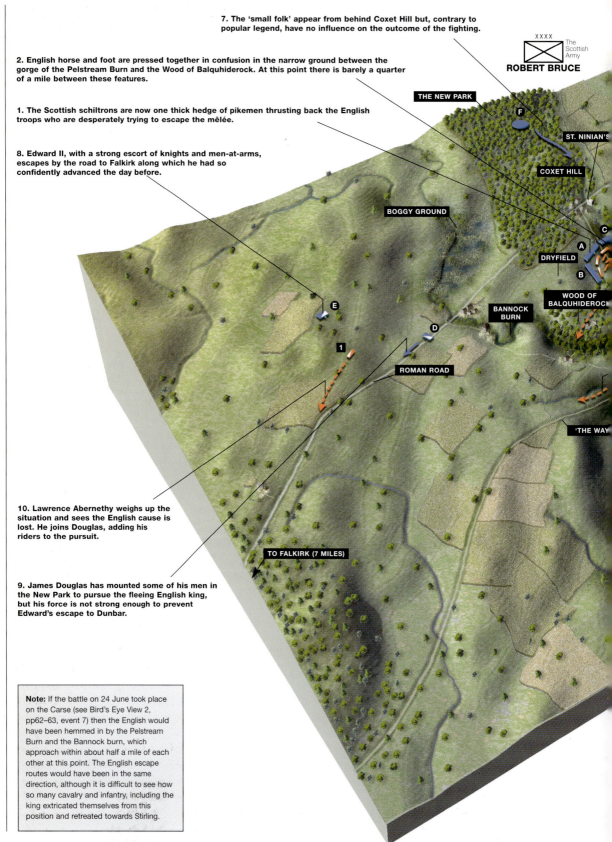

7. The 'small folk' appear from behind Coxet Hill but, contrary to popular legend, have no influence on the outcome of the fighting.

2. English horse and foot are pressed together in confusion in the narrow ground between the gorge of the Pelstream Burn and the Wood of Balquhiderock. At this point there is barely a quarter of a mile between these features.

1. The Scottish schiltrons are now one thick hedge of pikemen thrusting back the English troops who are desperately trying to escape the mêlée.

8. Edward II, with a strong escort of knights and men-at-arms, escapes by the road to Falkirk along which he had so confidently advanced the day before.

10. Lawrence Abernethy weighs up the situation and sees the English cause is lost. He joins Douglas, adding his riders to the pursuit.

9. James Douglas has mounted some of his men in the New Park to pursue the fleeing English king, but his force is not strong enough to prevent Edward's escape to Dunbar.

XXXX
The Scottish Army
ROBERT BRUCE

THE NEW PARK

ST. NINIAN'S

COXET HILL

BOGGY GROUND

DRYFIELD

BANNOCK BURN

WOOD OF BALQUHIDEROCK

ROMAN ROAD

'THE WAY'

TO FALKIRK (7 MILES)

A
B
C
D
E
F
1

Note: If the battle on 24 June took place on the Carse (see Bird's Eye View 2, pp62–63, event 7) then the English would have been hemmed in by the Pelstream Burn and the Bannock burn, which approach within about half a mile of each other at this point. The English escape routes would have been in the same direction, although it is difficult to see how so many cavalry and infantry, including the king extricated themselves from this position and retreated towards Stirling.

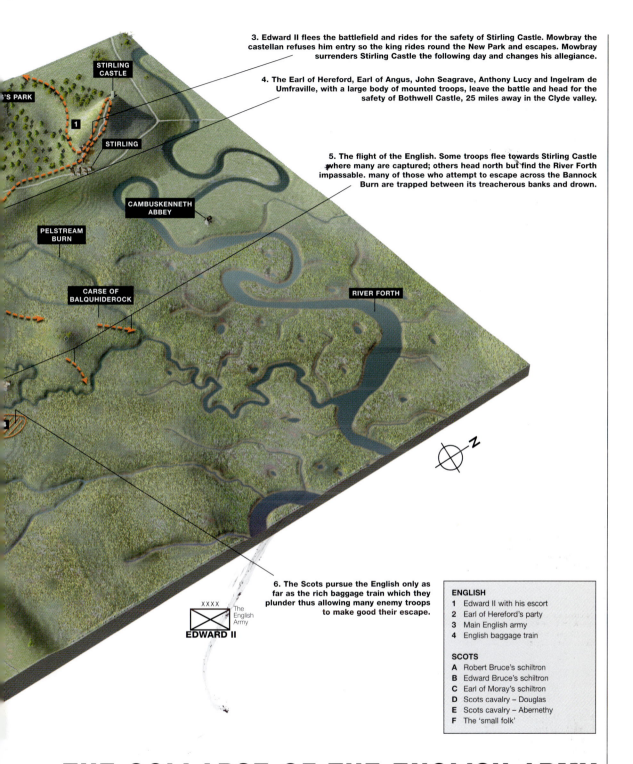

3. Edward II flees the battlefield and rides for the safety of Stirling Castle. Mowbray the castellan refuses him entry so the king rides round the New Park and escapes. Mowbray surrenders Stirling Castle the following day and changes his allegiance.

4. The Earl of Hereford, Earl of Angus, John Seagrave, Anthony Lucy and Ingelram de Umfraville, with a large body of mounted troops, leave the battle and head for the safety of Bothwell Castle, 25 miles away in the Clyde valley.

5. The flight of the English. Some troops flee towards Stirling Castle where many are captured; others head north but find the River Forth impassable. many of those who attempt to escape across the Bannock Burn are trapped between its treacherous banks and drown.

6. The Scots pursue the English only as far as the rich baggage train which they plunder thus allowing many enemy troops to make good their escape.

STIRLING CASTLE

'S PARK

1

STIRLING

CAMBUSKENNETH ABBEY

PELSTREAM BURN

CARSE OF BALQUHIDEROCK

RIVER FORTH

XXXX
The English Army
EDWARD II

ENGLISH	
1	Edward II with his escort
2	Earl of Hereford's party
3	Main English army
4	English baggage train

SCOTS	
A	Robert Bruce's schiltron
B	Edward Bruce's schiltron
C	Earl of Moray's schiltron
D	Scots cavalry – Douglas
E	Scots cavalry – Abernethy
F	The 'small folk'

THE COLLAPSE OF THE ENGLISH ARMY

Monday 24 June 1314, mid-late morning, viewed from the southeast. The English cavalry are repulsed by the Scottish pikemen and as their retreat turns to defeat and flight the King's banner is seen to leave the field. The infantry quickly follow suit, many not having struck a blow as they were behind the cavalry and hemmed in by the terrain. Only a fraction of the English army has been defeated but the Scots have won a great victory.

choked with the bodies of drowned men and horses that it could be crossed dry-shod.

When King Edward and his knights arrived before Stirling Castle they found that Sir Phillip Moubray had raised the drawbridge and barred the gates against them. Had Edward gained entry he would certainly have fallen into the hands of the Scots when the castle fell to the Scots, as it inevitably must in the aftermath of the battle. Moubray's action may have been because he foresaw this. Thus, and by good fortune, the King escaped. He rode around the King's Park, then across the rear of the Scots army before regaining the road through the Torwood, along which he had advanced with such confidence a short time before.

AFTERMATH

King Edward fled the battlefield accompanied by his favourite, Sir Hugh Despencer, whose expectation of the lands of the Earl of Moray were now dashed, and by Sir Henry Beaumont, whose quest for an earldom was, for the moment at least, disappointed. The Earl of Pembroke's retinue of knights and men-at-arms may have formed the rearguard and covered Edward's retreat. Pembroke's retinue suffered heavy casualties in the fighting, including Sir John Comyn, son of the 'Red Comyn' murdered by Bruce in Dumfries in 1306. The fugitives rode for the port of Dunbar and covered the 60 miles at such a pace that, as Barbour puts it, there was, 'not even leisure to make water'. Sir James Douglas set out in hot pursuit though he had fewer than 60 hastily gathered horsemen with him. As he rode through the Torwood he met Sir Lawrence Abernethy with 80 men who had come to help the English but, on seeing the situation, thought better of it and joined Douglas in the chase. Before they arrived at Linlithgow, the Scots came close enough to the fleeing English to

The ruins of Earl Patrick's castle stand guard over the entrance to the harbour at Dunbar. From here Edward II sailed for England at the end of his disastrous Bannockburn campaign. (photo Peter Ryder)

Graham Turner

exchange shouts of derision but Douglas judged them too strong to attack in the open. Barbour's assertion of the strength of Edward's force, which he puts at 500 men-at-arms compared to Douglas's and Abernethy's force, which numbered just less that 140 riders, may be an attempt to excuse his hero for his failure to prevent Edward's escape. Douglas nevertheless harried the English rearguard and picked off any stragglers. At Winchburgh the English halted and dismounted to rest their weary horses while Douglas followed suit close by. This is hardly the stuff of headlong flight; the halt at Winchburgh together with Barbour's description of Edward's prudently led and well-ordered men-at-arms, suggest an orderly withdrawal. Edward arrived at Dunbar on 25 June where the loyal Earl Patrick had a ship prepared that took the King safely to Bamburgh in Northumberland. Douglas, seeing that his efforts

John Comyn
Son of John Comyn "The Red" of Badenoch

John Lovel
of Tichmarch, Northants

William Lovel
of Norfolk

John de Hastings
of Bergavenney

John Gascelyn

John Mautravers

Philip Hastang

Aymer la Zouche
of Devon

William Vescy

Nicholas de la Beche

John Ryvere

Thomas Ercedekne

Thomas de Berkeley

Maurice de Berkeley

John Kingston

Nicholas Kingston

Bothwell Castle on the River Clyde has been called the grandest of Scotland's medieval castles. Edward I took it in 1301 with the aid of a huge siege tower called 'le berefrey' (belfry) that required 30 wagons to transport it from Glasgow. (photo Peter Ryder)

to take the King had failed, abandoned the pursuit and returned to Stirling. At Dunbar Edward's escort took the coast route to Berwick, which was about 25 miles away, and must have been back at that town by the evening of 26 June, just 11 days after they set out. The King rode up to Berwick from Bamburgh and spent the next two weeks there from 27 June.

When the English army broke up, a large numbers of soldiers, eager to escape the vengeance of the Scots, followed the King towards Stirling Castle where, unable to enter, they were cornered on the rocky outcrops below the castle. They posed a threat to Bruce's rear and he was forced to detach a strong body of men to contain them until they surrendered later in the day. Barbour blames the distraction caused by this incident, rather than any failure on the part of Bruce or Douglas, for the failure to mount an adequate pursuit of Edward II. The fleeing English troops were not pressed far beyond the Bannock Burn and, as soon as the remnants of the enemy under Stirling Castle had been dealt with, the Scots spent the rest of the day plundering the spoils of the battlefield and the English baggage train. The *Vita* tells us that 'while our people sought safety in flight, a great part of the Scottish army was occupied in plunder ... if all the Scots had been attending to the pursuit of our men, few would have escaped.'

Many English troops left the battle in some semblance of order, some had taken no part in the fighting and one English source records that 'over 200 knights neither drew sword nor struck a blow'. Sir Maurice Berkeley left the battle with a 'gret rout off Walis-men'. The Earl of Hereford 'with a great crowd of knights, six hundred other mounted men and one thousand foot, fled towards Carlisle'. At Bothwell Castle on the

Clyde, which was still in English hands, Walter Gilbertson, the castellan, admitted the Earl and 50 of his followers. Hereford made the mistake that the King had avoided at Stirling and found himself in a trap, for when Edward Bruce heard that the Earl was at Bothwell he gathered a strong force together and rode there without delay. When he appeared before the castle, Gilbertson, a Scot himself, abruptly changed his allegiance and opened the gates, surrendering the castle and with it the Earls of Hereford and Angus and a rich haul of barons and high-ranking knights.

The rest of the fugitives made their way up the Clyde Valley. They were still four days' march from the Border and ahead lay a tough 20-mile slog over the rough fells of the Southern Uplands into Annandale. The countryside was alerted and the population was in arms and hostile. Many of the fleeing troops would fall victim to the predatory Border clans of the area, who would snap at their heels all the way to the Solway Firth.

THE RECKONING – CAPTIVES AND CASUALTIES

The Earl of Hereford was the King's brother-in-law and was so rich a prize that Bruce exchanged him in October for 15 Scottish captives held in England. Among those released were Elizabeth, his Queen, his daughter Marjory, his sister Christina and Robert Wishart the Bishop of

The laird of Torthorwald was one of many Scots from south-west Scotland who fought for Edward II at Bannockburn; both he and the eldest son of his neighbour Dougal MacDowell were killed.

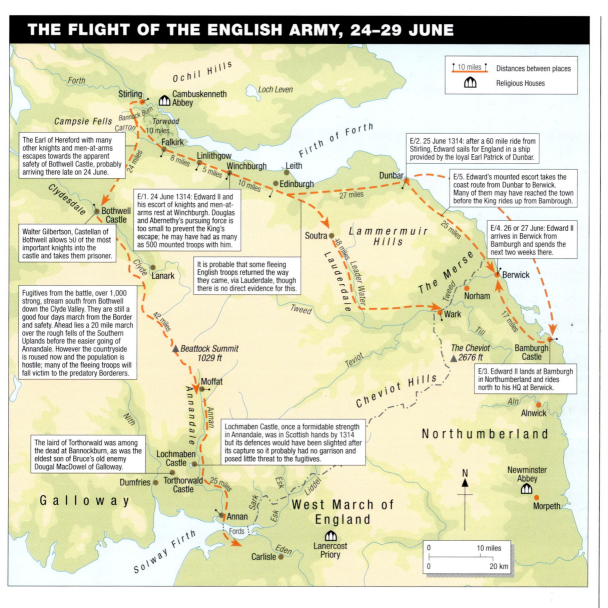

Ochil Hills

Forth

Campsie Fells

Loch Leven

Stirling
Cambuskenneth Abbey

Bannock Burn
Torwood
10 miles
Carron

Falkirk

Linlithgow
8 miles

Winchburgh
5 miles

Leith

Edinburgh
10 miles

Firth of Forth

Dunbar

27 miles

10 miles ↕ Distances between places
Religious Houses

E/2. 25 June 1314: after a 60 mile ride from Stirling, Edward sails for England in a ship provided by the loyal Earl Patrick of Dunbar.

E/5. Edward's mounted escort takes the coast route from Dunbar to Berwick. Many of them may have reached the town before the King rides up from Bambrough.

The Earl of Hereford with many other knights and men-at-arms escapes towards the apparent safety of Bothwell Castle, probably arriving there late on 24 June.

24 miles

Clydesdale

Bothwell Castle

Walter Gilbertson, Castellan of Bothwell, allows 50 of the most important knights into the castle and takes them prisoner.

Clyde

Lanark

E/1. 24 June 1314: Edward II and his escort of knights and men-at-arms rest at Winchburgh. Douglas and Abernethy's pursuing force is too small to prevent the King's escape; he may have had as many as 500 mounted troops with him.

Soutra

Lauderdale Leader Water

48 miles

Lammermuir Hills

25 miles

E/4. 26 or 27 June: Edward II arrives in Berwick from Bamburgh and spends the next two weeks there.

The Merse

Tweed

Norham

Berwick

It is probable that some fleeing English troops returned the way they came, via Lauderdale, though there is no direct evidence for this.

Tweed

Wark

Fugitives from the battle, over 1,000 strong, stream south from Bothwell down the Clyde Valley. They are still a good four days march from the Border and safety. Ahead lies a 20 mile march over the rough fells of the Southern Uplands before the easier going of Annandale. However the countryside is roused now and the population is hostile; many of the fleeing troops will fall victim to the predatory Borderers.

A72 miles

Beattock Summit
1029 ft

Annandale

Annan

Moffat

Teviot

Till

17 miles

The Cheviot
2676 ft

Cheviot Hills

Bamburgh Castle

E/3. Edward II lands at Bamburgh in Northumberland and rides north to his HQ at Berwick.

Aln

Alnwick

Northumberland

Nith

Lochmaben Castle, once a formidable strength in Annandale, was in Scottish hands by 1314 but its defences would have been slighted after its capture so it probably had no garrison and posed little threat to the fugitives.

Lochmaben Castle

The laird of Torthorwald was among the dead at Bannockburn, as was the eldest son of Bruce's old enemy Dougal MacDowel of Galloway.

Dumfries
Torthorwald Castle

Galloway

25 miles

Esk

Liddel

West March of England

Esk

Annan

Fords

Sark

Solway Firth

Eden

Carlisle

Lanercost Priory

N

Newminster Abbey

Morpeth

0   10 miles
0   20 km

Glasgow, who had grown old and blind during his long years of captivity. Bruce's nephew, Donald the young Earl of Mar, chose not to return as he had developed a close personal relationship with Edward II.

Ransom demands were huge and though there is no direct example of an earl's ransom from Bannockburn, we know that John de Bretagne, Earl of Richmond, who Bruce captured at Byland in 1322, paid the huge sum of £20,000 for his release. Sir Ralph Neville of Raby's son Robert, known as the 'peacock of the north', was captured at Bannockburn and freed by the Scots on security to procure a ransom of 2,000 marks (a mark was two-thirds of a pound sterling). The battle cost the Nevilles dear for Alexander and John Neville were also taken prisoner, leaving Lord Neville desperate for ways of raising the ransom. Sir Walter Fauconberg lost his eldest son at Bannockburn, his younger son was more fortunate, he was captured and ransomed for 500 marks. In November 1314 the King commanded the exchequer to pay Aleyn de

The shattered ruins of Kilton Castle in Cleveland, home of Sir Marmaduke de Thweng, are all that remain today to remind us of this famous old warrior.

Walingford, his sergeant-at-arms, the sum of £100 to ransom his son, who was also in the hands of the Scots.

Bruce regretted the death of his brother-in-law Gloucester, as well as the loss of his ransom, and had him taken to a nearby church where he maintained a vigil the night after the battle. The Earl of Gloucester and Sir Robert Clifford were the most prominent knights killed at Bannockburn and Bruce had their bodies returned to Berwick pickled in wine casks. The young Earl was eventually interred at Tewkesbury Abbey. Bruce showed humanity and generosity towards some of his prisoners. When Marmaduke de Thweng, hero of the battle of Stirling Bridge and many other encounters, surrendered to Bruce personally after spending the night after the battle hiding in a bush, he was treated like an old friend and sent home to Yorkshire ransom free. Sir Ralf Monthermer was freed without ransom too, which suggests the truth of the romantic tale of him having helped Bruce escape the anger of Edward I in his days at the English court. Not everyone was so fortunate to escape the wrath of the vengeful Scots, however, and we hear that Robert Bottel of Merstone's son 'lost both his ears by the violence of the Scots'.

Hundreds of horses and wagons loaded with stores and valuables were abandoned by the English and fell into the hands of the Scots. The great Privy Seal of England was discarded and found among the chaotic remains of Edward's machinery of government. The Carmelite Friar Robert Baston was discovered wandering on the battlefield; he was a notable poet of the day and King Edward had brought him along to immortalise his triumph over the Scots in verse. Instead, in return for his release, Bruce had him compose a poem to relate the Scots victory. It survives to this day, but unfortunately Brother Baston was more concerned with versifying than conveying information and his tedious Latin epic

contains little of factual value. Philip Moubray surrendered Stirling Castle the morning after the battle and was allowed to change his allegiance and come into King Robert's peace. The Scots, in line with their usual policy, immediately set about dismantling the defences of the castle.

It is impossible to estimate the casualties among the English foot, though losses would have been disproportionately spread as some units took no part in the fighting and may have withdrawn unscathed. The number of knights and barons killed at Bannockburn was quite astonishingly high by English standards of warfare. Casualty lists of the knighthood were usually short, as it was customary for a knight to surrender rather than be killed and prisoners were eagerly sought in battle as they brought a rich ransom. At the battles of Lewes and Evesham, within living memory, large bodies of baronial cavalry had fought together yet only a mere handful of knights had been killed. In previous affairs in Scotland the same had been true. Even at the disastrous battle of Stirling Bridge, which looms so large in folklore, apart from the unlamented Sir Hugh Cressingham few knights seem to have paid the price of Wallace's victory. The more fully documented battle of Falkirk the following year was fought on the grand scale, and though we know from the horse lists that numerous knights lost their mounts there is no evidence that the riders themselves suffered much damage.

Medieval chroniclers as a rule wildly overestimated the numbers of troops involved in battles, neither they nor their informants seem to have had a head for large numbers. Barbour was clearly out of his depth when he credits Edward with more that 100,000 fighting men. Yet when he writes of the number of English knights killed at Bannockburn he says that, 'Two hundred pairs of red spurs were taken from dead knights'. This is surely a sober and believable estimate. Barbour is at home with smaller numbers, particularly when he could probably enumerate many of the casualties by name. There exist, remarkably, two casualty lists for Bannockburn compiled shortly after the battle when interest in the disaster was at its height. The first is contained in the

ABOVE **Effigy of William Vescy of Malton in Yorkshire, who was 21 years of age when he was killed at Bannockburn. The effigy, like many of the memorials of Bannockburn, has suffered the ravages of time. It was originally in St Mary's Abbey in York but was removed and used as a parish boundary mark, being partially buried against a wall, thus inadvertently ensuring that the lower part remained in a fair state of preservation (re-drawn by the author from YAJ).**

ABOVE, LEFT **Roger de Woderington in Northumberland was a witness in court at a proof of age in 1335 and then aged 47 said that he was at Bannockburn with his lord Sir Robert de Bertram of Bothal Castle (above), who died there.**

SCOTTISH RAIDS ON NORTHERN ENGLAND, 1314–22

Edward Bruce 1314

6. 21 May 1318: Wark-on-Tweed Castle captured by the Scots.

5. 1–2 April 1318: Berwick captured by Sir James Douglas.

Berwick

Norham

Tweed

SCOTLAND

Teviot

Wark (30m, 40h)

Bamburgh (20m, 20h)

Cheviot Hills

1316

7. May 1318: Harbottle Castle captured by Scots.

Harbottle (45m, 120h between Harbottle & Prudhoe)

Aln

Alnwick (50m, 60h)

Warkworth (10m, 20h)

Northumberland

Liddesdale

Annan

Lochmaben

3. 22 July–1 August 1315: Carlisle besieged unsuccessfully by Robert Bruce.

North Tyne

Scaleby (10m, 30h)

Esk

Fords

West March

Lanercost Priory

April–May 1318 Moray & Douglas

Mitford

Wansbeck

Morpeth

8. May 1318: Mitford Castle captured by Scots.

Solway Firth

1315

S Tyne

Carlisle (130m, 200h)

Prudhoe

Newcastle (170m, 80h)

Tyne

Copeland

Cockermouth (12m, 20h)

Kirkoswald

Penrith

2. Destruction in the Eden Valley in 1314, Brough and Appleby burnt, though the castles there held out. Kirkoswald Castle destroyed.

Stanhope

Weardale

Wear

Durham

9. 1318: Hartlepool was a base for attacks against Scottish shipping. The town was attacked by the Scots as a reprisal for their activities.

Egremont

St Bees Priory

4. 1315: James Douglas raids Copeland and robs St Bees Priory.

Cumbrian Fells

Eden

Brougham (12m, 10h)

Appleby (30m, 20h)

Brough (15m, 20h)

1314

Teesdale

Barnard Castle

Tees

Hartlepool

1. 4 August 1314: As Edward Bruce's raiders return from plundering the prosperous north-eastern counties they are attacked on Stainmore by Andrew de Harcla and the Carlisle garrison.

Swaledale

Richmond

14. 20 October 1322: Battle of Old Byland, the English surprised and defeated by Robert Bruce, Edward II narrowly escapes capture and flees to Bridlington.

Furness Abbey

Cartmel Priory

Wensleydale

Ure

Swale

Northallerton

Old Byland

Rievaulx Abbey

Scarborough

10. 1318: Ripon was spared destruction by the Scots, as in 1316, on payment of a ransom of 1,000 marks.

Lancaster

Lune

Bowland Fells

Wharfedale

Thirsk

1322

Ripon

1322

Myton-on-Swale

1319

12. 1319: 'The Chapter of Myton', fought near Myton-on-Swale and so called because of the number of clerics killed in the skirmish.

Skipton

Boroughbridge

Knaresborough

York

Bridlington

Ribble

Airedale

Wharfe

Preston

Aire

13. 16 March 1322: Battle of Boroughbridge, Andrew de Harcla's victory over the rebel barons briefly revived Edward II's fortunes.

11. 1318: Knaresborough burnt by the Scots, 140 houses destroyed, only 20 left standing.

N

| 0 | | 20 miles |
| 0 | | 20 km |

Legend:
- Castle or walled town
- Peel/tower
- Religious Houses
- 12m — Men-at-arms in garrison 1316–17
- 20h — Hobelars

LEFT Cambuskenneth Abbey, scene of the treacherous Earl of Atholl's attack on the Scottish supply depot on the night of 23 June 1314.

chronicle known as the *Annals of London*, where the names of 37 knights killed at the battle are recorded. The second source is known as the *Continuation of Nicholas Trevet* and is a West Country chronicle of the years 1307–18. Here are listed the names of 80 of those killed and taken prisoner in the battle. The Earl of Gloucester heads the list, then follow the names of 27 of the barons and bannerets killed, of which

18 also appear in the *Annals of London*. The list continues with the names of 22 earls, barons and bannerets and 31 ordinary knights captured. The total of knights killed and captured according to Trevet was 154, over a hundred of whom are known to us by name.

There were losses among the Scottish knights too, though these were remarkably light, only William Vipoint and Walter Ross are named by Barbour as being killed in the battle. Edward Bruce was much distressed by Walter's death as he was the young brother of Isabella, daughter of the Earl of Ross, who Edward married in 1308. Sir William Airth was killed too, though in a curious aside to the battle. He was at Cambuskenneth, north of the River Forth, guarding the Scot's supply depot when, on the night of 23/24 June, the Earl of Atholl treacherously plundered the depot, leaving Sir William and a number of his men dead in their wake. Atholl's disaffection from the Bruce cause was because his sister Isabella had borne Edward Bruce an illegitimate son and was then it seems discarded by him in favour of the Ross marriage.

REASONS FOR THE ENGLISH DEFEAT

The battle of Bannockburn was a confrontation between Scotland's greatest warrior King and one of England's most unsuccessful and troubled Kings, who displayed little grasp of military realities. The Lanercost chronicler had no doubt who was to blame for the humiliating defeat, nor was he alone among contemporary commentators in laying the blame squarely on Edward II.

The English wrongly assumed that their initial advance along the high road from Falkirk would brush the Scots aside and that they would camp safely below Stirling Castle. Their plans were upset when they were

Robert de Reymes, whose effigy can be seen in Bolam Church in Northumberland, was taken prisoner at Bannockburn and paid a hefty ransom for his release. His misfortunes did not end there, for in the years following the battle Robert's Northumbrian estates were devastated by the Scots and the income from his lands fell from £50 a year to only 14s 7p.

twice repulsed on the 23rd, leading to the cavalry camping on the boggy carse with the infantry spread further afield. In effect the English had lost the initiative and were forced to spend the night dispersed widely and in an uncomfortable position that had no place in their plans. In the morning the Scots attack exploited the situation to the full, and the battle became an attempt by the English to fight their way out of a trap of their own making.

Edward brushed advice aside and may still have thought that the Scots would avoid a pitched battle on 24 June with the resulting confusion when they attacked at dawn. Tactics that demanded combinations of horse and foot were ignored. However, such tactics rely on subordination, organisation and firm leadership and, as these qualities were not on display at Bannockburn, they were probably not an option anyway. The lack of firm leadership allowed the arrogant and insubordinate baronial cavalry to assume the role that the socially superior knights demanded, while the infantry was relegated to a lesser role that was thought to befit their status. The superior numbers of the English should have tipped the balance in Edward's favour, but the restricted width of the battlefield where the English found themselves at dawn on the 24th, neutralised this advantage. Bruce's army was never confronted by the whole of the English army; the Scots defeated only a part of it yet it was enough to ensure victory. Crucially, the baronial heavy cavalry was beaten and their defeat proved decisive. Despite the assumptions of the knights, their headlong charge did not carry all before it and defeat quickly followed. As they were driven from the field before the Scottish pikes, the King fled for the safety of Stirling Castle and the infantry, many of whom had not even struck a blow, followed his example and fled in confusion.

The well-drilled Scottish schiltrons of pikemen were capably led by men that Robert Bruce knew he could trust to carry out his intentions. He was well aware of the capabilities as well as the vulnerability of unsupported pikemen, and he demonstrated during the battle that he knew how to use them both in a defensive role and in attack. The ineffective English leadership, in marked contrast, displayed no tactical notions other than attempting to use the heavy cavalry, quite unsupported by the infantry, to batter a way through the ranks of the Scots.

The greatest threat to the Scottish schiltrons were the English longbowmen but once the armies were locked together in close combat they needed to occupy a flanking position in order to shoot directly into the ranks of the Scots. They found themselves jammed into a tightly packed mass of men behind the English forward ranks of horsemen unable to shoot effectively or deploy because of the narrow confines of the battlefield. Blame for defeat at Bannockburn rests with Edward II but the victory undoubtedly belongs to Robert Bruce, who by his one signal triumph ensured his place as Scotland's greatest King.

RESULTS OF THE BATTLE – THE LONG WAR CONTINUES 1314–28

With his overwhelming victory Robert Bruce established himself in a position of unassailable authority as King of Scots and won the

The Tile Tower and part of the City Walls of Carlisle. In 1315 Robert Bruce besieged the town, and despite the use of siege machines the garrison held out, losing only two men. All the Scots achieved was to trample down the cornfields and drive off the livestock.

OPPOSITE The arms of Sir Robert de Reymes, displayed at Bolam Church, Northumberland.

independence of Scotland even though the English stubbornly refused to accept these facts. If the Scots had been able to mount a more effective pursuit after the battle and if the Earl of Dunbar had acted like Walter Gilbertson at Bothwell then Edward II might have been captured. As it was, the escape of the hapless English King made victory incomplete and a peace settlement proved elusive. Bannockburn marked the low point of Edward's unfortunate reign but it was not the end of his misfortunes as Scottish raids across the Border became so frequent that they practically amounted to the subjection of England, north of the River Tees, to the Scots. Northumberland was reduced to anarchy not only by the depredations of the Scots but also by those of predatory local garrisons and robber bands. Many of the people of Cumberland and Northumberland despaired of relief from the English government and became 'Scottish', just as many in the Lothians had previously been 'English'. Large areas of the northern counties were subjected to selective devastation and were forced to buy the Scots off with payments of 'blackmail', which further fuelled the Scottish war effort. In July 1315 King Robert boldly laid siege to Carlisle, but the town held out due to a well-conducted defence organised by Sir Andrew Harcla. In April 1318 Berwick, the only Scottish town to remain in enemy hands after Bannockburn, was betrayed to the Scots and taken by Sir James Douglas. The fall of Berwick was a severe blow to the English and its loss was compounded by the fall of the Northumbrian castles of Wark-on-Tweed, Harbottle and Mitford. In May that year a Scottish raid struck deep into Yorkshire and burnt Northallerton, Boroughbridge and Knaresborough and terrorised the citizens of Ripon, who bought them off with a payment of 1,000 marks.

In a desperate bid to salvage his pride, Edward II joined forces with his adversary Earl Thomas of Lancaster and laid siege to Berwick but met with no success. Moray and Douglas, with a force of 8,000 men, raided deep into Yorkshire in a bid to distract Edward from the siege. The mayor and Archbishop of York raised such men as they could and

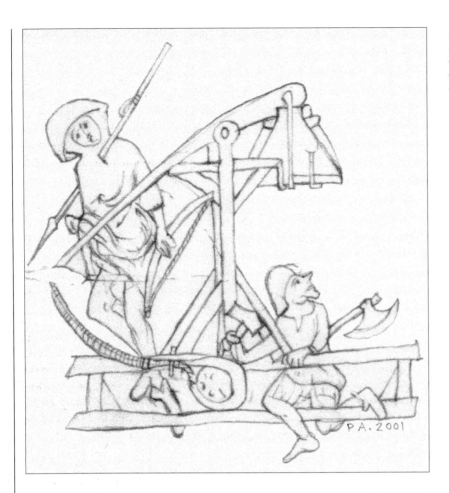

marched out to confront the marauding Scots. At Myton-on-Swale their motley force was soundly defeated by the Scots in an unequal affair known as the 'Chapter of Myton' because of the large number of clergymen killed and captured. Edward raised the siege of Berwick and retreated south of the River Trent, allowing the Scots to ravage Cumberland and Westmorland unmolested. In December the English negotiated a two-year truce but a long-term peace was still far off because of Edward's arrogant refusal to relinquish his claims of sovereignty over the Scots. In 1320 the Scots addressed the famous Declaration of Arbroath to the Pope in which they made it clear that Scotland was and always had been an independent kingdom. Subsequent peace talks in 1321 ended in deadlock again. Later that same year relations between Lancaster and his adherents and the King and his favourites the Despencers deteriorated into civil war. In March 1322 the rebel barons were defeated by Sir Andrew Harcla at the battle of Boroughbridge, which resulted in Lancaster's capture and execution.

With his position strengthened for the time being Edward led what was to be his last expedition into Scotland in August 1322. The English marched through Lothian as far as Edinburgh but hunger soon forced them to retrace their steps as the Scots withdrew before them, leaving anything of use to the invaders in flames behind them. As Edward retreated south, Robert Bruce led a strong mounted raiding force across the Solway and down the Eden Valley into North Yorkshire. At

Northallerton, on hearing that Edward was at Rievaulx Abbey 15 miles away, Bruce and his men rode without delay for the Abbey hoping to capture the English King. At Old Byland the Scots found their way blocked by John of Brittany, Earl of Richmond, with a considerable English force. Without delay Douglas and Moray dismounted their men and launched a spirited attack up the hill on which the English were posted. At the same time King Robert and his highlanders climbed what must have seemed impassable crags to the English and established themselves in a flanking position from where their wild charge swept the startled enemy before them. Edward was warned of his danger and for the second time he narrowly escaped capture but was again forced to abandon his personal equipment, silver plate, jewellery and horse trappings as he fled. The affair was not a disaster on the scale of Bannockburn but for Edward the humiliation of repetition was even greater. In 1323 a new Anglo-Scottish truce was agreed that was intended to last for 13 years, but final peace was to come only after further warfare. Edward II was deposed on 20 January 1327 and his 14-year-old son was crowned as Edward III on the first day of February. A council of regency was established to rule the country headed by Henry, the new Earl of Lancaster, though the influence of the Queen mother, Isabella, and her lover Mortimer pervaded the new government. In the summer a hugely expensive campaign in Northumberland, which ended with the embarrassing fiasco of Stanhope Park, failed to check the renewed onslaught of the Scots on the North of England. The situation was desperate as it seemed that this time Bruce intended to occupy demoralised Northumberland and parcel out lands there to his men. Isabella and Mortimer considered war but, fearful of the backlash of defeat, they chose instead to make peace. By the terms of the treaty of Edinburgh that concluded the long war the English finally renounced all claims of sovereignty over Scotland. It was a remarkably fair and statesmanlike settlement and 'it would indeed have been well for both countries if the agreement of 1328 had governed the relations of the two countries for the rest of the middle ages'. But it was not to be as the belligerent young Edward III reopened hostilities within five years and a new phase of the Scottish Wars began.

MILITARY TACTICS AFTER BANNOCKBURN

Bannockburn established the military ascendency of the Scots over the English that was maintained for the rest of King Robert's reign. The battles of Myton-on-Swale in 1319, Old Byland in 1322 and the affair of Stanhope Park in 1327 inflicted humiliating reverses on the English. These were small-scale affairs that relied on surprise, mobility and the mercurial leadership of Bruce and his lieutenants for their success. The Scots leaders nevertheless knew that the victory at Bannockburn had been due to a combination of pikemen, archers and light cavalry acting in concert on favourable ground and continued to exploit this knowledge. King Robert died in 1329, James Douglas was killed in Spain in 1330 and with the passing of Moray in 1332 the Old Guard was no more. The lesson of Bannockburn became clouded and the Scottish leadership put their faith in the unsupported charge of the schiltrons of pikemen alone. But the English, who had learned the hard way, had learned well, as Sir Andrew Harcla demonstrated at Boroughbridge in 1322. Harcla dismounted his knights and men-at-arms and formed them into a schiltron, flanked by archers. The Lanercost chronicler observed at the time that Harcla fought in the 'Scottish fashion', but soon this irresistible combination of archers and dismounted men-at-arms would become known as the English manner of fighting. When Edward III ascended the throne of England in 1328 war was soon resumed with the Scots, who realised to their cost that it was the English that had taken the lessons of Bannockburn to heart. Never again were the ill-disciplined English cavalry to charge headlong on to the pikes of the Scottish schiltrons. The Scottish debacle at Dupplin Moor in 1322 was not only a forerunner of the even greater disaster of Halidon Hill the following year but heralded years of defeat at the hands of the English. At Halidon Hill the fully-developed tactical combination of archers and dismounted knights and men-at-arms, in a carefully chosen position and led by the King himself, came into its own. The onslaught of the schiltrons of pikemen stalled in the face of the storm of arrows from the wedges of English bowmen and with their ranks decimated they recoiled and fell back as the English men-at-arms remounted and charged, turning bloody defeat into a headlong rout. English battlefield tactics had in less than 20 years evolved into a battle-winning formula that would be repeated in France during the Hundred Years War. The Scots, meanwhile, had forgotten the lessons of Robert Bruce and the years of victory.

BANNOCKBURN THEN AND NOW

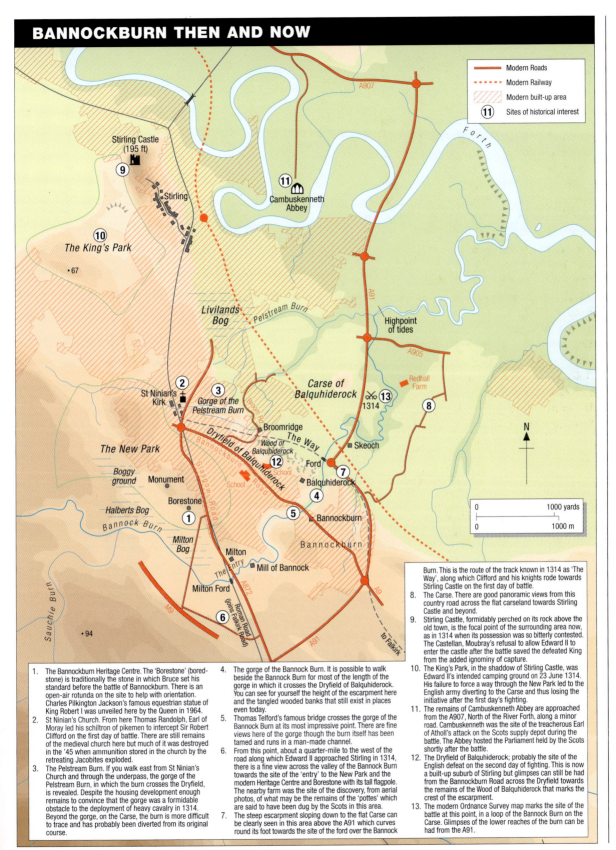

Legend:
- Modern Roads
- Modern Railway
- Modern built-up area
- (11) Sites of historical interest

Stirling Castle (195 ft) (9)

Stirling

(11) Cambuskenneth Abbey

Forth

(10) The King's Park

• 67

Livilands Bog

Pelstream Burn

Highpoint of tides

Carse of Balquhiderock

Redhall Farm

(2) St Ninian's Kirk

(3) Gorge of the Pelstream Burn

Broomridge

The Way

(13) 1314

(8)

The New Park

Dryfield of Balquhiderock

Wood of Balquhiderock

Skeoch

Boggy ground   Monument

(12)

Ford

(7)

Halberts Bog

Borestone

(1)

School

(5)

Balquhiderock

(4)

Bannockburn

Milton Bog

Milton Entry

Bannock Burn

Bannockburn

Sauchie Burn

Milton

Mill of Bannock

Milton Ford

(6)

Roman Road (joins Falkirk Road)

Glasgow Road

to Falkirk

• 94

N

| 0 | | 1000 yards |
| 0 | | 1000 m |

1. The Bannockburn Heritage Centre. The 'Borestone' (bored-stone) is traditionally the stone in which Bruce set his standard before the battle of Bannockburn. There is an open-air rotunda on the site to help with orientation. Charles Pilkington Jackson's famous equestrian statue of King Robert I was unveiled here by the Queen in 1964.
2. St Ninian's Church. From here Thomas Randolph, Earl of Moray led his schiltron of pikemen to intercept Sir Robert Clifford on the first day of battle. There are still remains of the medieval church here but much of it was destroyed in the '45 when ammunition stored in the church by the retreating Jacobites exploded.
3. The Pelstream Burn. If you walk east from St Ninian's Church and through the underpass, the gorge of the Pelstream Burn, in which the burn crosses the Dryfield, is revealed. Despite the housing development enough remains to convince that the gorge was a formidable obstacle to the deployment of heavy cavalry in 1314. Beyond the gorge, on the Carse, the burn is more difficult to trace and has probably been diverted from its original course.
4. The gorge of the Bannock Burn. It is possible to walk beside the Bannock Burn for most of the length of the gorge in which it crosses the Dryfield of Balquhiderock. You can see for yourself the height of the escarpment here and the tangled wooded banks that still exist in places even today.
5. Thomas Telford's famous bridge crosses the gorge of the Bannock Burn at its most impressive point. There are fine views here of the gorge though the burn itself has been tamed and runs in a man-made channel.
6. From this point, about a quarter-mile to the west of the road along which Edward II approached Stirling in 1314, there is a fine view across the valley of the Bannock Burn towards the site of the 'entry' to the New Park and the modern Heritage Centre and Borestone with its tall flagpole. The nearby farm was the site of the discovery, from aerial photos, of what may be the remains of the 'pottes' which are said to have been dug by the Scots in this area.
7. The steep escarpment sloping down to the flat Carse can be clearly seen in this area above the A91 which curves round its foot towards the site of the ford over the Bannock

Burn. This is the route of the track known in 1314 as 'The Way', along which Clifford and his knights rode towards Stirling Castle on the first day of battle.
8. The Carse. There are good panoramic views from this country road across the flat carseland towards Stirling Castle and beyond.
9. Stirling Castle, formidably perched on its rock above the old town, is the focal point of the surrounding area now, as in 1314 when its possession was so bitterly contested. The Castellan, Moubray's refusal to allow Edward II to enter the castle after the battle saved the defeated King from the added ignominy of capture.
10. The King's Park, in the shadow of Stirling Castle, was Edward II's intended camping ground on 23 June 1314. His failure to force a way through the New Park led to the English army diverting to the Carse and thus losing the initiative after the first day's fighting.
11. The remains of Cambuskenneth Abbey are approached from the A907, North of the River Forth, along a minor road. Cambuskenneth was the site of the treacherous Earl of Atholl's attack on the Scots supply depot during the battle. The Abbey hosted the Parliament held by the Scots shortly after the battle.
12. The Dryfield of Balquhiderock; probably the site of the English defeat on the second day of fighting. This is now a built-up suburb of Stirling but glimpses can still be had from the Bannockburn Road across the Dryfield towards the remains of the Wood of Balquhiderock that marks the crest of the escarpment.
13. The modern Ordnance Survey map marks the site of the battle at this point, in a loop of the Bannock Burn on the Carse. Glimpses of the lower reaches of the burn can be had from the A91.

91

APPENDIX

'The history of England is enshrined in our Parish Churches'.

Effigies, tombs and monuments of those who fought at Bannockburn
The list is not exhaustive and the subject would repay further research:

King Edward II, tomb and effigy, Gloucester Cathedral.
The Good Sir James Douglas, tomb and effigy, Douglas, Lanarkshire.
Robert de Reymes, effigy and heraldry, Bolam, Northumberland.
Robert Neville, 'The Peacock of the North', effigy, Brancepath, Co. Durham.
Gilbert de Clare, Earl of Gloucester, Window, Tewkesbury Abbey, Glos.
William Vescy, effigy, York Museum.
Aymer de Valence, Earl of Pembroke, tomb and effigy, Westminster Abbey.
Edmund Mauley, effigy, Bainton, Yorks.
Robert Mauley, formerly in York Minster now destroyed, drawing in *Archaeologia* xxxi.
Thomas Berkeley, effigy, Bristol Cathedral.
Maurice Berkeley, effigy, Bristol Cathedral.
Nicholas Leybourn, effigy, Calder Abbey, Cumbria.
Anthony de Lucy, effigy, Berwick, St John.
Alan/Aymer la Zouche, effigy, Forthampton Court, Glos.
Nicholas Stapleton, effigy, Kirkby Fleetham, Yorks.
Henry Percy, effigy, Fountains Abbey, Yorks.
Gerard de Lisle, tomb, Stowe-Nine-Churches, Northants.
Gifford, effigy, Boyton, Wilts.
John Mauleverer, effigy, Allerton Mauleverer, Yorks.
Warin de Scargill, effigy, Darrington, Yorks.
Robert Ryther, effigy, Ryther, Yorks.
Roger Tyrell, effigy, Dilwyn, Hereford.
John, 2nd Baron Hastings, effigy, Abergavenny, Gwent.

LEFT **The arms of Sir Robert Clifford, displayed on an ancient building in Appleby, remind visitors to the old town of its Clifford connections.**

SELECT BIBLIOGRAPHY

Primary Sources

Scalacronica by Sir Thomas Grey of Heton, trans. Sir Herbert Maxwell (Glasgow, 1907)
The Chronicle of Lanercost, ed. & trans. H. Maxwell (Glasgow, 1913)
Vita Edwardi Secundi monachi cuiusdam Malmesberiensis; the life of Edward II by the so-called Monk of Malmesbury, ed.& trans. N. Denholm-Young (Nelson's Medieval Texts, 1957)

Secondary Sources

Armstrong P. *The Battle of Bannockburn, Heraldry, Armour and Knights* (Lynda Armstrong Designs Pubs., 1998)
Barbour J. *The Bruce*, ed. A.A.M. Duncan (Edinburgh, 1997)
Barrow G.W.S. *Robert Bruce and the Community of the Realm of Scotland* (London, 1965)
Christison Gen. Sir Philip *Bannockburn, A Soldier's Appreciation of the Battle* (National Trust for Scotland, 1960)
MacDonald W.R. *Scottish Heraldic Seals* (Edinburgh, 1904)
Mackenzie W.M. *The Battle of Bannockburn, A Study in Medieval Warfare* (Glasgow, 1913; reprinted, Strong Oak Press, 1989)
McNair Scott R. *Robert the Bruce, King of Scots* (Edinburgh, 1982)
McNamee C. *The Wars of the Bruces* (East Linton, 1997)
Morris J.E. *Bannockburn* (Cambridge, 1914)
Oman Sir Charles *A History of the Art of War in the Middle Ages Vol.II* (Greenhill Books, reprinted 1991)
Reese P. *Bannockburn* (Edinburgh, 2000)
Scott W. *Bannockburn Revealed*, (Rothesay, 2000)
Traquair P. *Freedom's Sword* (London, 1998)
The Complete Peerage, xi Appendix B

Helmet and crest of the King of Scots. The mantling bears the arms of Robert Bruce's lordship of Annandale. (author's drawing from the Armorial de Gelre)

INDEX

95